The
Business Wisdom of
Ancient Chinese Entrepreneurs

The Business Wisdom of Ancient Chinese Entrepreneurs

TIMELESS PRINCIPLES FOR MODERN TIMES

SOO BOON HONG

PARTRIDGE

| ISBN: | Softcover | 978-1-4828-6703-9 |
| | eBook | 978-1-4828-6704-6 |

Print information available on the last page.

To order additional copies of this book, contact
Toll Free 800 101 2657 (Singapore)
Toll Free 1 800 81 7340 (Malaysia)
orders.singapore@partridgepublishing.com

www.partridgepublishing.com/singapore

CONTENTS

INTRODUCTION

Fan Li aka Tao Zhu Gong and his 12 Principles of Business

The journey of a thousand miles begins with a single step.

—Lao Tzu

Fan Li aka Tao Zhu Gong was the author of the greatest business treatise (The 12 Business Principles of Business). He was a contemporary of Sun Tzu, the author of the great ancient Chinese military treatise on war. Both were from the era of the Warring States in ancient China over more than 2500 years ago. Sun Tzu with his 13 chapters of war has shaped and molded the thinking of strategists from its inception till now. Consisting of **6075 Chinese characters**, The Art of War by Sun Tzu has presented a stable and timeless system of strategic thinking in military campaigns and competitive scenarios. Unknown to the world, Tao Zhu Gong's 12 Principles of Business is the complete business system for the ancient and modern Chinese.

The Chinese worshipped Fan Li as one of the sages in business. His 12 Principles of Business rivals Sun Tzu's Art of War in completeness and eloquent simplicity. Giving us the essence of each principle in 3 Chinese words, Fan Li's original completed treatise was a total of **36 Chinese characters** (12 principles times 3 words per principle), yet within them contained the whole world of entrepreneurship.

To demonstrate the relevance of Tao Zhu Gong's powerful principles, we can examine the 6th Principle which deals with being compensated and the financial sphere of the business, should any company fails to secure its rightful compensation or fails in establishing a healthy financial state, it will inevitably fail. This principle is relevant today and will continue to be so into the future. By mastering Tao Zhu Gong's 12 Principles, the reader is equipped with a "compass" to navigate the abundant but deadly seas of business.

From its inception, well-meaning scholars of previous centuries added their definitions, business lessons and pitfalls to streamline the immensely varied and creative aspects of Tao Zhu Gong's work. This book focuses on the original 3 character script, hence returning to the original meaning of Tao Zhu Gong.

Bai Gui and His 4 Characteristics of Successful Entrepreneurs

Bai Gui, a native from the state of Zhou, in ancient China during the era of the Warring States, was the founder of the first recorded business school in ancient China. He was a business-savvy, decisive, moral, responsible and self-disciplined entrepreneur. Bai Gui's timeless contribution was the 4 Characteristics (graphically represented in the matrix in his chapter) that he deemed necessary for his potential students to have before he considered them worthy to be admitted into his business school.

From these 4 aspects, we learn that to be a successful entrepreneur requires more than just blind hardwork and luck. In the 2009 America subprime financial crisis, the banks and individuals involved in the whole financial mess fulfilled 3 out of 4 of Bai Gui's 4 Characteristics, failing on the 3rd Characteristic of Compassion (inclusive of integrity and morals). Even after over 2 thousand years, Bai Gui's basic and yet critically important 4 human character requirements still ring true today.

Bai Gui's 4 Characteristics help the readers to identify and define the critical areas to rectify and strengthen to build a successful, enduring and prosperous enterprise.

The Graphical Matrix System

The ancient Chinese possessed a way of delving deep into the heart of the issue, realizing that everything is interconnected at deep levels in intricate yet harmonious systems.

Sun Tzu, in his manuscript on the art of war, simply stated the essentials to consider in each chapter dealing with each different yet critical aspect of waging war. Likewise Tao Zhu Gong's 12 Principles of Business gives us the 12 business systems or in Warren Buffett's terminology; 12 circles of competence, for his readers to build upon and adapt to the nature of their enterprises.

The considerations that went into the matrix designs are:

1. These matrices are the products of the ***author's understanding and interpretations*** of the interactions and influences of the basic business factors.

2. **"A picture is worth a thousand words"** as the old saying goes, hence by presenting the basic factors in a visual manner, it is easier to see the interconnectedness and whereby the paths of influence interact between different factors.

3. **Providing the readers with a conceptual framework of the critically important and universally present business factors that are relevant to that chapter in a beautifully designed graphical conceptual map.**

4. **In no way are the matrices complete and comprehensive for all the varied and complex business systems of the world.** The readers are encouraged to build their own designs

like *Toyota* which built a diagram encompassing all its values and principles to guide its organization and stakeholders.

5. Within each factor of the matrix, there are many facets to reveal the intricacies of things. Like a good diamond, the more facets it has, the more sparkles it has when light is shone on it. **The readers are encouraged to explore their chosen entrepreneurs and enterprises in the space provided in "POWERFUL"** *P:*Person *O:*Organization *W:*What Challenges *E:*Executions *R:*Results *F:*Factors of Success/Failure *U:*Understanding *L:*Lessons

The human mind thinks in images and other modes of information, rarely does any great breakthrough comes in the form of words. Albert Einstein achieved his breakthroughs on the speed of light and relativity by imaging himself riding on a beam and travelling through space at light speed. The creation of benzene came to its creator via a dream of a serpent biting its tail. Even the epic musical scores of Beethoven came to him in blocks of music playing in his head. It is with this understanding that the author is emboldened to take a new path in the presentation of business concepts.

The Macro, Micro and 13 Strategic Aspects for Clarity

Multiple shades of meanings exist simultaneously in the ancient Chinese style of writing. It is up to the readers' levels of wisdom and experience to discover, decipher and interpret the meanings generating a wide array of views and understanding. Success depends on getting the complete picture.

The Big Pictures/ the Macro Views/ the Big Spheres of Influence

It is the broad view of things. Like the view of the audience viewing a theatrical play, the audience can see all the actors and actresses performing together.

In the competitive business environment, the macro view is similar to viewing how all the enterprises and their competitors interact on the "stage" of the industry for survival and success.

In the enterprise, the macro view is similar to viewing how all the different departments of the enterprise interact on the "stage" to produce the vital performances needed.

Perspectives/ the Micro Views

The micro view is the examination of the issue from multiple angles.

In the competitive business environment, the micro view is the performance of the individual component/department on a stand-alone basis.

In the enterprise, the micro view is the performance of the enterprise in all the vital business activities.

13 Strategic Aspects

The timeless principles discussed in this book deal with the various big spheres in which all enterprises must engage proactively in.

These 13 strategic aspects represent the 13 areas that the entrepreneur must consider in the application of the business principles.

Together with the graphical matrices, they help form a conceptual framework for the entrepreneurs to expand and build upon, gaining mastery over these principles.

How *NOT* to use this book

Even Sun Tzu cannot guarantee and ensure that his readers will become accomplished strategists and generals from reading his legendary book of war. Throughout the ages, millions have read his book; all will gain strategic insights and depth in handling various situations yet the level of success achieved by each individual is dependent solely on the skillful applications and masterful adaptions of his principles of war to the ever-changing circumstances. Hence the following:

1. The reader's character, capabilities and principles (the TZG 1st Principle Matrix presents this inner world), the mastery and skill in applying Tao Zhu Gong's 12 Principles will determine the level of success. **In the domain of knowledge and experience, there are no substitutes or shortcuts for the processes of assimilation by the readers through their own exposures, efforts and experiences.**

2. There are no X-steps to success in this book, there are only powerful and timeless principles for the determined and ambitious readers to master and apply.

3. The graphical matrices are based and designed to the **author's broad interpretations** of the teachings of the ancient Chinese entrepreneurs in the **author's micro view/perspectives.**

4. **The readers are encouraged to build their own matrices based on the applications of the business principles and to adapt to the unique business environments they operate in.**

白圭
bái guī

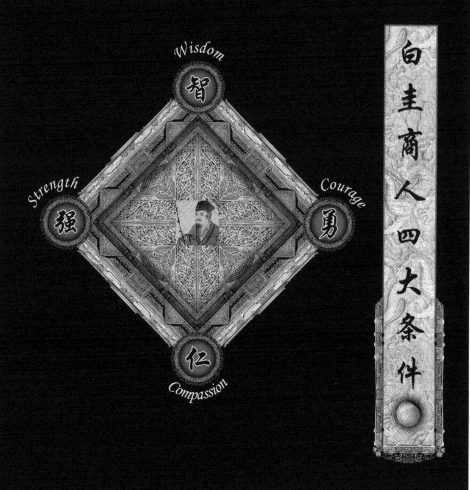

Bai Gui's 4 Characteristics of Successful Entrepreneurs.

Bai Gui—Founder of the First Business School in Ancient China

A principle is a principle.
And in no case can it be watered down because of our incapacity to live it in practice.
We have to strive to achieve it, and the striving should be conscious, deliberate and hard.
—Mahatma Gandhi

Bai Gui（白圭）

Bai Gui was revered by modern Chinese as "商祖", meaning the forefather of business. His name was recorded into the Chinese historical annals in the segment on famous entrepreneurs.

Like a rare diamond amongst the rocks, Bai Gui's brilliance was his founding of the first recorded business school in ancient China and the immortal example of being a successful socially responsible entrepreneur. His name and deeds were recorded for future generations to learn of his wisdom and principles; a worthy role model for the ages.

Bai Gui became wealthy from the trade in grains, the raw materials, tools and finished products of artisans, segments of the market that were shunned by many business people due to the significantly lower returns compared to other more lucrative businesses like mining or luxury items.

Li Bu Wei (李不韦), the wealthy merchant who sponsored the exiled Prince of Qin, Yi Ren (异人), who eventually succeeded the Qin State. Prince Yi Ren married Li's concubine and their son became the legendary Qin Emperor who united China. Li once asked his father about the profit margins in the various businesses. His father revealed that to trade in agricultural products, one can make 10 times profit (if you invest 1 dollar, you will get 10 dollars back); peanuts compared to the vast profits of antiques and precious luxury goods with a margin of 100 times.

Bai Gui had demonstrated the soundness of his business principles by becoming immensely wealthy from the less lucrative and fiercely competitive business of trade in agricultural products. His wealth accrued was comparable to the richest men in that region.

6

Sima Qian (司马迁) a famous Chinese historian whose work covered a span of 2000 years of Chinese history chronicled Bai Gui into his work, *The Records of the Grand Historian* 《史记》, under the section about merchants and business (货殖列传). Sima Qian praised Bai Gui for his business acumen and stood witness as Bai Gui's teachings were spread down the ages via his deeds and students.

Bai Gui emphasized that businessmen could be compassionate and moral and yet earn their rightful share provided they provide their customers with wholesome products and good value. Using his own success as example Bai Gui showed that it is possible to be a moral, compassionate businessman and be successful at the same time.

One of his many methods to benefit the people was in the way he purchased grain and various food stocks. The vast majority of China's population during that era consisted of peasants and craftsmen. During the autumn harvests, Bai Gui would stockpile vast quantities of *relatively lower grade food grains* and *good quality seeds* at cheap prices due to the oversupply in the market.

During the spring replanting seasons, when the reserves of food grain began to be depleted. Bai Gui would resell these peasants and craftsmen the lower food grade grains at a very thin profit margin for consumption (this is not fraud as it will be explained shortly). Peasants and craftsmen were not affluent during that era, and they cared little about the taste or texture of their food grain as long they were ensured of a full stomach. Demand for cheap grain was relatively inelastic and the demand was great and the customers for these lower grade grains knew what they were getting. Bai Gui made his fortune by looking after the poorer peasants and craftsmen. Compared to other unscrupulous merchants who raised prices of all types of grains to fully take advantage of the people during a difficult period.

During the replanting phase in spring, Bai Gui would resell the good quality seeds that he bought cheaply last autumn at a very modest price to the peasants. He believed that once farmers had access to cheap and abundant good seeds, they were assured of increased yields and good harvests down the following months, the food supply in the market would be abundant and everyone would benefit. With enough food stocks, the local and surrounding population would increase, ensuring more potential customers for the businessmen to serve.

Bai Gui taught his students that the interests and well-being of the merchants must be tied to the interests of society at large. He particularly despised merchants who cheated their customers, believing that such unscrupulous people were harming society and inevitably harming themselves in the process.

Sima Qian categorized merchants into two categories. Merchants like Bai Gui who were benevolent and selfish merchants who cared only for profits. Sima Qian stated that selfish merchants would earn about 30% profit from their trading while benevolent ones would produce a higher profit of roughly 50%.This has to do with the trading styles in the past eras. Greedy merchants were overzealous in their pursuit of profits, were calculative and fretting over each transaction. Armed with skills of timing the market, these merchants in the short term seemed to profit a lot. According to Sima Qian, in the long term, the benefits and advantages gained by the greedy merchants were not huge.

Benevolent merchants did not seek vast and easy profits. They were not greedy and desired only huge volume of trade with thin profit margins, earning little from each transaction. With their sterling reputations, they enjoyed strong customer support and hence their trading cycles were much faster that greedy merchants'. Resulting in faster return of investment and profits to reinvest, in the long term, the gains were significant.

Bai Gui was a frugal, disciplined and diligent entrepreneur and shunned the luxuries of life easily afforded by his immense wealth. He was a hardworking boss, working alongside with his many workers. At the same time, a wise teacher imparting his business acumen in a business school that he set up. His student selection criteria was simple (4 Characteristics) and yet profound (vast applications).Bai Gui considered these four characteristics as absolutely essential in the potential candidate, without which their learning of business from him would be a futile and fruitless endeavor. The 4 Characteristics are presented in the Bai Gui's Matrix.

The Bai Gui Matrix (BG Matrix)

The BG Matrix is read in the following order: Wisdom, Courage, Compassion and Strength.

For the modern entrepreneurs especially in the search for talents and capable people to grow their companies, these 4 Characteristics represent the bare basics that a potential candidate must have. Bai Gui's powerful set of criteria can aid in people selection ranging from CEO selection to the selection and training of distributors in multi-level marketing by the simple promise that any violation will result in mediocre results or worse, disaster for the enterprise with dire consequences.

 Wisdom

It does not take sharp eyes to see the sun and the moon,
nor does it take sharp ears to hear the thunderclap.
Wisdom is not obvious.
You must see the subtle and notice the hidden to be victorious.
—Sun Tzu, The Art of War

According to Bai Gui, wisdom in the context of business is the ability to discern opportunities and adapt to the ever changing conditions of the business world.

Characteristic in Action

(**P**erson)

(**O**rganization)

(**W**hat Challenges)

(**E**xecution)

(**R**esults)

(**F**actors of Success/Failure)

(**U**nderstanding)

(**L**essons and insights)

The Aspects of Wisdom to Consider:

- o   Pragmatic
- o   Logical
- o   Intuitive
- o   Balanced and equilibrium
- o   Macro view/ Overview
- o   Micro view/ Detailed view
- o   Changes occurring with time
- o   Changes occurring with different experiences
- o   Speed and agility in thinking.
- o   (Reader's Insights)

The Essence: Wisdom is the state of mind without folly and folly is the state of mind lacking wisdom. Know the difference and see the world in new empowering perspectives.

 Courage

The first duty of man is to conquer fear;
he must get rid of it, he cannot act till then.

—Thomas Carlyle

According to Bai Gui, courage is defined as the state of mind to act decisively when opportunities arise.

Characteristic in Action

(**P**erson)

(**O**rganization)

(**W**hat Challenges)

(**E**xecution)

(**R**esults)

(**F**actors of Success/Failure)

(**U**nderstanding)

(**L**essons and insights)

The Aspects of Courage to Consider:

- o   The mastery over fears and doubts.
- o   The overall view of how events or decisions fit into the big picture
- o   The manifestation of grace under fire
- o   The ability to strategize and execute plans courageously.
- o   (Reader's Insights)

The Essence: Courage must augment good strategy in order to be fearless in face of obstacles on the path to success. The demands of strategy must harness and guide courage to be instrumental in its deployment, lest overzealous courage leads to unwarranted actions that jeopardize the whole campaign.

 # Compassion

Compassion is the basis of all morality.

– Arthur Schopenhauer

Bai Gui's definition of compassion is that the entrepreneurs' drives for profits must be tempered with wisdom and integrity, for the entrepreneurs' actions do impact society.

Characteristic in Action

(**P**erson)

(**O**rganization)

(**W**hat Challenges)

(**E**xecution)

(**R**esults)

(**F**actors of Success/Failure)

(**U**nderstanding)

(**L**essons and insights)

The Aspects of Compassion to Consider:

- o Compassion
- o Wisdom
- o Morals
- o Integrity
- o Responsibility
- o Balance
- o (Reader's Insights)

The Essence: Great compassion was found in the acts of Bai Gui and Tao Zhu Gong. Tao Zhu Gong would donate great portions of his immense wealth during times of famine and flood to alleviate the sufferings of the victims. He cared for the people more than his wealth, in his heart; wealth was nothing but a tool to aid people.

# Strength

In reading the lives of great men,
I found that the first victory they won was over themselves...
self-discipline with all of them came first.

— *Harry S Truman*

In the teachings of Bai Gui, strength does not mean power or skill; he used the word to represent the fortitude in self-discipline. To him, there is no strength greater than the discipline of self and the reining in of desires.

Characteristic in Action

(**P**erson)

(**O**rganization)

(**W**hat Challenges)

(**E**xecution)

(**R**esults)

(**F**actors of Success/Failure)

(**U**nderstanding)

(**L**essons and insights)

The Aspects of Strength (Self Discipline) to Consider:

- o Identification of weaknesses in self.
- o Mastery of weaknesses with an iron will supported by effective techniques
- o Joy in the self-betterment process
- o Superb emotional controls
- o Balance in the levels of self-discipline.

o   Wisdom to know what and when and how to control with regards to desires for pleasures.
o   (Reader's Insights)

The Essence: Self-discipline is like the level of tension in the strings of musical instruments; know the optimum level to bring forth the perfect note.

陶朱公
tao zhū gōng

The 12 Business Principles of Tao Zhu Gong

Fan Li aka Tao Zhu Gong— the Sage of Business

Simplicity is the ultimate sophistication

—Leonardo da Vinci

Fan Li / Tao Zhu Gong

Fan Li (范蠡), a famous statesman, strategist and entrepreneur who lived during the era of the Warring States in ancient China. He was a native of the state of Chu and was born around 536 BC.

He and his friend Wen Zhong (文种) entered into the service of the state of Yue, under the King of Yue, Gou Jian (勾践). Fan Li's statesmanship and governing skills were instrumental in aiding Gou Jian to rebuild and strengthen the state of Yue after a disastrous and devastating military defeat at the hands of its old neighbor and enemy, the state of Wu.

Decades later, the state of Yue managed to destroy its arch enemy and became a power house in the surrounding region. Fan Li and Wen Zhong were elevated to the highest official positions in the country, enjoying immense power and wealth.

Fan Li, knowing the character of Gou Jian and the perils of such lofty positions and power, warned his friend Wen Zhong to leave as soon as possible. Wen Zhong refused to leave as he could not believe that Gou Jian would eliminate them after having they had contributed and sacrificed so much. Fan Li made the necessary preparations before he petitioned for retirement with Gou Jian in the Imperial Court of Yue. True to form, Gou Jian cajoled, pleaded and later threatened Fan Li and his entire family with death for wanting to leave. Gou Jian could not imprison Fan Li for suggesting early retirement and Fan Li's great contributions to the state of Yue stayed Gou Jian's hand long enough for him to escape with his family. Wen Zhong was ordered to commit suicide for a trumped up charge by Gou Jian not long after Fan Li's escape.

Fan Li and his family journeyed to the state of Qi, settling down near the seaside, they began to rebuild their shattered lives. Using the pseudonym of 鸱夷子皮 (chi yi zi pi), Fan Li and his family worked the barren lands, growing agricultural products and rearing livestock. Capitalizing on their proximity to the sea, they began to venture into fishing and the harvesting of salt from the seawater. Within a few years, Fan Li achieved great wealth which attracted the attention of the King of Qi who did not know Fan Li's true identity. Sending an imperial emissary to Fan Li, the King of Qi offered him the position and imperial seal of the Prime Minister of his state. Such was the admiration the King of Qi had for Fan Li's abilities.

Upon learning of the intentions of the King of Qi, Fan Li sighed and remarked that possessing great wealth and the offer of Premiership to a commoner like him were ominous signs of things to come. He returned the seal and immediately gathered his friends and people from the surrounding areas. Fan Li distributed his considerable wealth amongst them, especially towards the poor and needy. Taking only some money and valuables as seed capital, Fan Li and his family again left under the cover of night and travelling along the remote pathways out of Qi.

Fan Li studied the teachings of 道 (Tao/Dao or The Way of Nature). In nature, he observed that anyone or anything that reaches and passes its zenith, decline is inevitable. A fruit once ripe will begin to decay and rot. A flower once blooms in beauty, will fade and wilt. In the state of Yue, he achieved the highest position enjoying great wealth and power. Fan Li realized that unless he voluntarily diminished himself, the cycle of nature would inevitable force him into decline or disaster. Likewise in the state of Qi, Fan Li felt that he had reached his zenith, disaster and decline would follow shortly.

Travelling to the bustling region of Tao (陶), he settled down and adopted the pseudonym of Zhu Gong (朱公), soon people were addressing him as Tao Zhu Gong (陶朱公). Beginning all over again, Fan Li and family soon achieved a level of wealth so great that people ranked him as the richest man in China during that time. And his pseudonym was used as a title for the extremely wealthy in the future generations.

What made Fan Li truly great were his charitable deeds, he would aid the needy, the poor, widows and orphans with his immense wealth. Leaving sufficient money to meet his family's needs, Fan Li would use up all his great wealth to aid and alleviate the suffering of the people during times of severe disasters. Within a few years, Fan Li would again regain his wealth, a testament to his genius in the sphere of business. Sima Qian praised Fan Li for being a rare role model for the ages, being wealthy and at the same time able to bestow charity and aid on such a wide scale.

Fan Li's sharp business acumen was crystalized into his treatise of business 陶朱公商训, *The Business Principles of Tao Zhu Gong* and passed down the generations. 12 business principles in total (each consisting of 3 characters, a total of 36 characters) for the future generations of entrepreneurs to build upon to meet the business challenges of their time eras.

After his passing, the Chinese people deified him as a God of Wealth, due to the rapid speed at how he managed to earn back his wealth despite his multiple and vast donations and for his generous and compassionate nature.

Sadly, with the passage of time, the modern Chinese have little or no impression of Fan Li/Tao Zhu Gong. When they think about praying to him, they focused on getting wealth through prayers, instead of learning his powerful principles and great noble spirit. Worse still, many are not even aware such a great and noble person existed.

This book seeks to introduce these great ancient Chinese entrepreneurs and their timeless principles to the modern era in hope to inspire a new generation of great entrepreneurs.

The Subtleties behind the Words

The three characters located in the red circles are his actual words. The ancient Chinese language differs from the modern version in its simplicity and yet a single word on its own can possess an array of shades of meanings.

Using the TZG 1st Principle, 能识人 (neng shi ren) as an example.

能 (neng) as an adjective, it denotes the capability to do something. As a noun, it means the possessing the skill to do something, in the modern Chinese 能力 (neng li) is used in the same measure but with 力 (li) power added to add clarity.

识(shi) as a verb, means to know, recognize (认识ren shi), or to see through a ploy (识破shi po).

人 (ren) is a noun meaning human or a adjective denoting the state of humanness人性(ren xing) meaning human nature. Fan Li could also mean人类 (ren lei) the human race, 人品 (ren ping) the level of cultivation in a person, 人格 (ren ge) the character of an individual.

Put together能识人 (neng shi ren) can mean the ability to know, recognize and understand people, their characteristics and their strengths and weaknesses.

能识人(neng shi ren) if interpreted on a superficial level is not much different from a resume (which narrowly deals with skills related to vocation). The level of experience, the amount and type and depth of exposure, the years of interacting with people, the cultural influences of people in contact are all significant factors which add new perspectives and dimensions to the one's understanding of people.

The significance of placing能识人 (neng shi ren) as the first principle showcases its vital importance. Another perspective is the understanding of the various positive and negative factors that could affect people and influence their business interactions with you.

陶朱公商训第一则　能识人

Tao Zhu Gong's Business Principle 1: The Ability to Know People

THE FIRST BUSINESS PRINCIPLE—
THE ABILITY TO KNOW PEOPLE

Knowing others is intelligence; knowing yourself is wisdom.
Mastering others is strength; mastering oneself is true power.

—Lao Tzu

The Business Essentials—People

The concept of business is entirely a human product. Humans from ancient times engaged in trade to satisfy the needs, wants and desires even until now and will continue to do so into the distant future. All business activities stem from the needs, wants and desires of people. Businesses move to satisfy them, and in the process earning a profit and ensuring the survival of the enterprise.

Change is a permanent factor in all strategic considerations and planning. Entrepreneurs have capitalized on the flux of change to achieve growth and prosperity. The ability to master change is a critical skill that the entrepreneurs must cultivate and augment. One of the keys to mastering change is having the people in the enterprise be committed, loyal and capable in rising to the challenges that change brings.

Throughout history, spanning from the ancient eras to the modern times, countless leaders of empires, countries and business enterprises succeeded and failed via their choice of people to be placed in positions of great importance.

The critical first step is the ability to know people well. Only by knowing people well, could the entrepreneurs/enterprises be able to realize the full potential of their human resource and utilizing it for the success of the enterprise.

The 13 Strategic Aspects

1. Understanding and Analysis
- *The clarity of self and others.*

2. Acquisition of Information
- *The keen observations of self and others.*

19

3. The Battle Environment
- *The minds of people.*

4. Topography of the Environment
- *The inner aspects to be discovered.*

5. Weakness and Strength
- *The discoveries, augmentation and elimination for improvement.*

6. Commitment
- *The entrepreneur's drives and reasons in mastering this principle.*

7. Strategic Planning
- *The strategies, tactics and methods to discover the attributes.*

8. Preparation
- *The preparations for the strategies and tactics used in the discovery and utilization of such knowledge.*

9. Competitive Advantage
- *The use of the entrepreneur's competitive advantage(s) to discover.*

10. The Maneuvers
- *The understanding forged from the deciphering the observations with the principles of psychology and sociology.*

11. The Engagement
- *The careful observations of the individuals over a range of situations and tests.*

12. The Leadership
- *The determination of the motives and drives of the individual.*

13. Change and Adaption
- *The understanding of change and its impact on the individual.*

The Matrix of Tao Zhu Gong's 1st Business Principle (The Core Matrix)

As an entrepreneur, salaried professional or a freelancer, you need to know yourself well (represented by the purple cores in the matrix) to be able to understand in relation to other people, to the society, to the business you are engaged in, to the products/services you are selling and more so as to be poised to achieve greater heights. The matrix will help you systematically decipher the mysteries and subtleties of the human heart.

The central core represents the foundation for all the other "rings" to build upon.

Reading the matrix from the centre outwards, there are 4 vital rings/zones:

1. The 心 Heart core.

2. The 6 Aspects of Self (purple-colored factors)

3. The 8 Aspects of Observation (blue-colored factors)

4. The 3 Aspects of Deed (red-colored factors)

Organizations are a collective reflection of the people running them, seemingly to possess human traits and a "personality" to some extent. The author uses the word "individual" or "person" to treat the company or organization as a human entity for the ease for writing. It depends on the reader's perspective of applying the principles on a personal level or at an organizational level.

The Heart 心

"心" is the Chinese word for the heart, located in the center of the matrix. Like the English word, it has 2 meanings, the physical heart and the metaphysical heart (emotions, beliefs, faith etc.). The ancient Chinese valued self-mastery and self-discipline in order to achieve the state of being a 君子 (jun zi), a noble and superior person by means of virtues and cultivation. The human heart, it is the soul of the individual. All of us are familiar with the thoughts generated but where is the *source* that originates the thoughts?

Even if a telepathic person is to read others, he/she could only read the thoughts generated, the telepath could not predict accurately the trends of the thoughts nor the next thought unless he/she knows the individual well (which does not guarantee a higher degree of accuracy). The stirrings of the heart are likened to the wind. Moving air is invisible but not nonexistent; we can feel the light breeze and see the physical effects wrought by wind. The thoughts generated within us come into being and vanished without a trace. This is the inherent unpredictable nature of the heart.

From the pages of history throughout the world, human kind seems to be trapped in an endless cycle, doomed to repeat certain lessons over and over again. Revealing the potential brilliance and follies of humanity has remained fairly constant from the distant past to the modern era. Noble, evil and mundane are the nature of our thoughts. The mastery of the heart through sustained effort and time will produce magnificent results, giving us deep insights and awareness into ourselves, others and the world.

The *6 aspects of self* (the innermost ring of purple factors) provide a basic foundation for us to build upon the understanding of self and of others. The *8 aspects of observation* (the middle ring of blue factors) provide a clear cut system to identify, measure and analyze the character of a person. Lastly, the *3 aspects of deed* (the outermost ring of red factors) reveal to the world, the subtle inner workings of the individual. By mastering the wonderful and rare ability to read people, the reader is able to adapt to the various situations and people encountered in business and being able to make decisions from a position of wisdom and power.

The 6 Aspects of Self (Purple Factors)

The depths of the individual are revealed via these 6 purple factors. The differences between individuals are:

1. The *types* of qualities present in each aspect; wholesome/good or unwholesome/evil.

2. The *intensity* of the qualities present in each aspect; strong or weak.

3. The individual's *mastery* over the qualities; nonexistent, normal or great.

The 8 Aspects of Observation (Blue Factors)

These 8 aspects of observation are derived from the writings of Zhuge Liang (诸葛亮), the Prime Minister of the Kingdom of Shu during the era of the Three Kingdoms in the history of ancient China. During a critical phase of his wildly successful first military campaign against the Kingdom of Wei, Zhuge Liang selected the wrong candidate to hold their critical path of retreat and the Shu army was almost annihilated.

Losing the campaign and all the hard fought cities, the Shu army retreated. Zhuge Liang reflected on his mistakes and his weaknesses, resulting in a treatise on the ways to gauge a person. The main factors in the blue circles represented the areas to analyze. People change with time and experiences, Zhuge Liang's treatise offered a basic template for reading a person.

The 3 Aspects of Deed (Red Factors)

The 3 aspects of deed represent the end phase of the individual's mental, emotional, intuitive and spiritual inner processes. By observing these 3 aspects over a wide range to situations, we can approximately gauge the inner workings (6 aspects of self) of the individual.

The ability to know people well is still the most elusive skill that the entrepreneur has to master. With the aid of the core matrix, the entrepreneur has a conceptual framework to build up his/her people reading skills.

 # Characteristics

A man's character is his fate.

– Heraclitus

Characteristics are defining qualities that separate an individual, culture, groups of people from another. In the realm of invisible or vague characteristics, using the example of identical twins to illustrate, purely identical in every biological aspect but each possessing different characteristics. Therefore each twin treading different life paths and forging different destinies.

The crux is the beliefs the one possesses that drive the changes in characteristics of the individual. No one is born perfect. An individual can strive to possess as many wholesome characteristics as humanly possible by modeling good role models from the histories and modern era. Hence the influence of the unwholesome characteristics must be controlled, reduced and mastered. Otherwise they may become formidable hindrances to one's success.

By striving to achieve the opposites of what are mentioned in the points below, you will achieve a deeper understanding of yourself. Only you alone can do this, for no one else can.

Principle in Action

(**P**erson)

(**O**rganization)

(**W**hat Challenges)

(**E**xecution)

(**R**esults)

(**F**actors of Success/Failure)

(**U**nderstanding)

(**L**essons and insights)

The Aspects of Characteristics (A Negative Mirror) to Consider:

- o Lacking in an understanding of self.
- o Lacking in strength and convictions.
- o Lacking self-mastery and self-discipline.
- o Lacking in the ability to adapt.
- o Lacking the means to observe, analyze and understand the ever-changing environments and circumstances. (Chapter 10 matrix presents the main areas where the change could manifest.)
- o Lacking in the ability to 'make things happen".
- o Lacking effective, efficient and economical in executional abilities.
- o Lacking in the ability to grow.
- o Lacking the strategic vision to adapt to the fast changing circumstances.
- o Lacking the foresight to understand the future of things given the current trends..
- o (Reader's Insights)

The Essence: Strength and weakness are the two sides of a coin. The situation and context will determine what strength is and what weakness is. Augment your strengths and crush your weaknesses.

 # Principles

In matters of style, swim with the current;
In matters of principle, stand like a rock.

—Thomas Jefferson

Principles are the individual's rules for guiding his/her actions. Principles and character share a self-reinforcing dynamic; by adhering to the noble principles even a base character can become noble. For it takes strength of character to commit to the good principles in the first place.

Clear principles and commitment to uphold them play an overwhelming role in guiding you well when you are in a chaotic situation, where disorder reigns and emotions run high. The ability to think coolly and strategically in such situations rests on the foundation of strong principles.

Be warned, like the yin and yang, there are misguided and vicious principles existing in the world and in all eras. You must examine what are your principles, where and how they become accepted by you, for your principles will lead you to success or to ruin.

Principle in Action

(**P**erson)

(**O**rganization)

(**W**hat Challenges)

(**E**xecution)

(**R**esults)

(**F**actors of Success/Failure)

(**U**nderstanding)

(**L**essons and insights)

The Aspects of Principles to Consider:

- **Relationships**: Principles about your actions in relation towards self, family, society, country and world.
- **Flexibility**: Principles about the actions that you may encounter and/or need to engage in as the situation and circumstances change.
- **Execution**: Principles in you that guide your actions as you rise up to challenges and responsibilities that are ever-present in life.
- **Adaption**: Principles guiding how you would prepare or react whether change appears slowly or drastically.
- **Material**: Principles on handling the physical objects (visible and tangible objects like properties, money down to a paperclip or a blade of grass) and invisible ones (invisible but existing like goodwill, reputation etc.)
- **Selection**: Principles guiding you on the selection of other principles.
- **Growth**: Principles guiding your growth.
- (Reader's)

The Essence: Be clear on your principles, where you stand and why.

 Values

Your beliefs become your thoughts.
Your thoughts become your words.
Your words become your actions.
Your actions become your habits.
Your habits become your values.
Your values become your destiny.

— *Mahatma Gandhi*

Our beliefs help us interpret the world we live in. Our principles serve as a guide for our thoughts and actions. Actions repeated successfully and regularly forge habits. Reinforced habits become values (automatic templates for actions used by the individual in the course of living).

A thrifty person is one who is *having the values* that limits unnecessary expenditure. First and foremost, to become a thrifty person, you must have beliefs that convince you to embrace the virtues of thrift. Your will need some congruent principles and planning to put your beliefs into action. As you progress, cutting out unnecessary spending and building up a sizeable bank account, your actions become easier and more automatic. Over time the habits of spending wisely will become second nature and you have a value of thrift.

Two different people may share the same values of thrift. On the surface, it looks the same, in reality subtle differences exist; only in the understanding of the beliefs and observing the execution of the value can one have a more accurate picture. Candidate A is thrifty due to the fact that he/she grew up in a financially challenged household directly influencing his/her spending habits, while Candidate B grew up in a wealthy household. What makes Candidate B thrifty? The answer is in the beliefs on money held by Candidate B. One is forced by circumstances and the other empowered by the beliefs held.

Principle in Action

(**P**erson)

(**O**rganization)

(**Wh**at Challenges)

(**E**xecution)

(**R**esults)

(**F**actors of Success/Failure)

(**U**nderstanding)

(**L**essons and insights)

The Aspects of Values to Consider:

o   Having a clear and accurate assessment of your values/beliefs.
o   Understanding how your values/beliefs are formed.
o   Realizing the true impact of your values/beliefs.
o   Awareness of the benefits and liabilities of upholding a particular value/belief.
o   Understanding the metrics you are using to measure the effectiveness of your values/beliefs.
o   Understanding the foundations of your values/beliefs.
o   Under what conditions will these foundations change and how will you reformulate a new value/belief?
o   Having the methods and resources to identify a self-limiting value/belief and to eradicate it.
o   Having any good role models to learn from.
o   (Reader's Insights)

The Essence: Your beliefs are the starting point of your destiny. Ensure that you have reflected on the end results of your beliefs before engaging them.

 Strengths

"Strength does not come from physical capacity.
It comes from an indomitable will."

– Mahatma Gandhi

Strengths in the context of this factor are the skills/advantages that the individual possesses. Strengths are context and situation-based. A skill/ability or possession of a vital resource in a situation makes it a strength/strategic advantage *if* others lack it or pale in comparison. Strengths are relative. They exist in comparison to what others have or have not.

Principle in Action

(**P**erson)

(**O**rganization)

(**W**hat Challenges)

(**E**xecution)

(**R**esults)

(**F**actors of Success/Failure)

(**U**nderstanding)

(**L**essons and insights)

The Aspects of Strength to Consider:

- o   Identifying your areas of strengths.
- o   Knowing the foundations of your strengths? (e.g. natural flair, constant and innovative practice sessions and more)
- o   Knowing the areas in which your strengths can be used to achieve success.
- o   Discovering the limits of your strengths.
- o   Understanding and mastering the factors affect the 'power' and sustainability of your strength.
- o   Maintaining your strength for optimal performance.
- o   Controlling the circumstances/timing/environment that affects the performance of your strengths.
- o   The factors affecting the relevance of your strength in the present and future.
- o   The innovation of your strengths to produce new levels of advantageous growth.
- o   (Reader's Insights)

The Essence: Strengths being developed to the extremes can become weaknesses, for great dependency on the strengths may result in an overreliance upon them.

Weaknesses

"Anything cracked will shatter at a touch."

—Ovid

Weaknesses are flaws that the individual/team/organization possesses. Anything that obstructs and hinders in the achievement of success can be used to discover the presence of any hidden weaknesses. More importantly the way you or your team/organization handles the challenge will reveal flaws. It is best that you crush your weaknesses before your opponents can use it against you.

Principle in Action

(**P**erson)

(**O**rganization)

(**W**hat Challenges)

(**E**xecution)

(**R**esults)

(**F**actors of Success/Failure)

(**U**nderstanding)

(**L**essons and insights)

The Aspects of Weakness to Consider:

o   Types of weakness revealed/discovered.
o   Viewing the weakness in the context of the macro view/big picture view of your life and its affected areas.
o   Realizing the costs of indulging in the weakness in terms of quality of life, peace of mind, potential success lost or in monetary terms.
o   Discovering the sources of weakness.
o   Correct analysis and identification of the real issues behind the weaknesses.
o   Having a clear, result-focused commitment to minimize and eliminate the weakness.

    o   Having a positive alternative to substitute the weakness if possible.

    o   (Reader's Insights)

The Essence: Discover your weaknesses, learn what factors form and support them and eradicate them without mercy.

 # Transformations

"What we achieve inwardly will change outer reality."

—Plutarch

Transformations are the changes wrought when the individual encountered new events, people and ideas, potentially altering the current inner world to the benefit or detriment of the affected individual. Transformations can be self- induced from insights gained.

<u>Principle in Action</u>

(**P**erson)

(**O**rganization)

(**W**hat Challenges)

(**E**xecution)

(**R**esults)

(**F**actors of Success/Failure)

(**U**nderstanding)

(**L**essons and insights)

<u>The Aspects of Transformation to Consider:</u>

    o   Discovering the critical transformation triggers that invoke significant change in the individual.

    o   Understanding the types of change wrought and its implications.

o   The viability of the transformations.
o   The trend of the transformation.
o   The speed of the transformation process.
o   The requirements and costs of the transformation.
o   The sustainability of the transformation. What factors augment or debilitate it?
o   (Reader's Insights)

The Essence: People change.

 # Ambitions

"Intelligence without ambition is a bird without wings."

–Salvador Dalí

Ambitions represent the dreams and goals of the individual that he/she aspires to achieve in his/her lifespan. Observations on this aspect of the individual will reveal the inner direction and the strength of the drives that propel him/her to achieve.

Principle in Action

(**P**erson)

(**O**rganization)

(**W**hat Challenges)

(**E**xecution)

(**R**esults)

(**F**actors of Success/Failure)

(**U**nderstanding)

(**L**essons and insights)

The Aspects of Ambition to Consider:

o   Discovering the ambitions.
o   Understanding the drives and reasons of the individual to attain and realize the ambitions.
o   The plans, preparations, strategies and tactics devised and deployed in the realization of the goal.
o   Presence of internal qualities that will aid or hinder the fulfillment of the ambitions.
o   Controllable or uncontrollable desire to achieve it? Passion or obsession?
o   Possessing the requisite skills or resources to attain his/her ambitions?
o   Having the ability to handle the changes wrought while in the pursuit of his/her ambitions.
o   The nature of the ambition itself. Good or evil?
o   (Reader's Insights)

The Essence: Everyone possesses ambitions. It is the manner the individual plans, prepares and initiates to achieve his/her ambitions that is revealing. The nature of the ambitions reveals the moral fabric of the individual inner world.

Gauge by: Question and cast doubts on the individual to measure the depth of his/her conviction towards his/her ambitions.

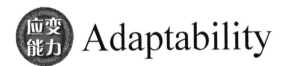 # Adaptability

*"I have always believed, and I still believe, that whatever good or bad fortune may come our way
we can always give it meaning and transform it into something of value."*
—*Hermann Hesse*

In human sphere, adaptability is the ability to control and master the effects of change to meet the objectives of the individual. If a living organism cannot adapt, it will perish and disappear from this plane of existence.

Principle in Action

(**Person**)

(**Organization**)

(**W**hat Challenges)

(**E**xecution)

(**R**esults)

(**F**actors of Success/Failure)

(**U**nderstanding)

(**L**essons and insights)

The Aspects of Adaption to Consider:

o   Understanding from the macro and micro perspectives of the impact and implications of the changes.
o   Investigate the limits of the new effects coming into play.
o   Discovering the new conditions for success after the old ones have been negated.
o   Seeking out advantages in the new environment to survive and prosper.
o   Avoiding pitfalls and dangers.
o   (Reader's Insights)

The Essence: Adapt or die.

Gauge by: Making (or observing in instances where attempts to irritate the individual) the individual irritated and angry to learn what he/she responds to and the manner in which he/she responds. Do not put your career at risk in order to gauge this aspect of your peers or superiors. Let them reveal in time.

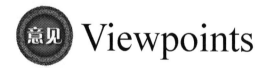 # Viewpoints

> *It is our attitude toward events, not events themselves, which we can control.*
> *Nothing is by its own nature calamitous even —death is terrible only if we fear it.*
> *— Epictetus*

Viewpoints are the views of the individuals on the discussed topic, person or event.

Principle in Action

(**P**erson)

(**O**rganization)

(**W**hat Challenges)

(**E**xecution)

(**R**esults)

(**F**actors of Success/Failure)

(**U**nderstanding)

(**L**essons and insights)

The Aspects of Viewpoint to Consider:

- o The types of viewpoints presented.
- o The ideas behind the viewpoints.
- o The stand/stance/position taken by the speaker.
- o The perspectives and angles explored in the viewpoint.
- o The strategic values in the viewpoint.
- o The experience of the individual with respect to the topic discussed.
- o (Reader's Insights)

The Essence: If one has nothing good to say, say nothing at all.

Gauge by: Noting the range of topics discussed with the individual, in various settings to test and ascertain depth of knowledge.

 Courage

Although the world is full of suffering,
it is also full of the overcoming of it.

– Helen Keller

Courage represents the bravery of the individual facing challenges or difficult situations. Courage in a sense is defined by fear. Courage is needed to break through the cage of fear imposed.

Principle in Action

(**P**erson)

(**O**rganization)

(**W**hat Challenges)

(**E**xecution)

(**R**esults)

(**F**actors of Success/Failure)

(**U**nderstanding)

(**L**essons and insights)

The Aspects of Courage to Consider:

o   The types of courage shown by the individual.
o   When is the courage revealed?
o   Where is the courage present?
o   Why is the courage summoned?
o   Who is/are involved?
o   What is/are to be done and the role of courage in the task(s)?
o   Instilling the right values and perspectives can produce moral courage.
o   Understanding the strategic and tactical view from the big picture forms the foundation for patient courage.
o   Understanding the nature of fears paired with effective and ample training will produce courage.
o   (Reader's Insights)

The Essence: Courage is putting fear in its rightful place and role as a *guide*.

Gauge by: Measure the levels of courage by deeds and actions of the individual not by words.

 修养 Cultivation

Men's natures are alike;
it is their habits that carry them far apart.

— *Confucius*

Cultivation represents the level of inner character refinement that the individual has and the subsequent training or efforts being put into its development or the lack of it. Cultivation cannot be gauged from superficial appearances and actions.

Principle in Action

(**P**erson)

(**O**rganization)

(**W**hat Challenges)

(**E**xecution)

(**R**esults)

(**F**actors of Success/Failure)

(**U**nderstanding)

(**L**essons and insights)

The Aspects of Cultivation to Consider:

- o   The level of cultivation present in the individual.
- o   Your first impressions and the variance in these impressions over time.
- o   The amount of time spent in observation and verification.
- o   The whole picture of the individual's actions, speech and thoughts may give a rough representation of the level of cultivation within.
- o   Time reveals everything.
- o   Deceivers cannot stand the test of time.
- o   (Reader's Insights)

The Essence: Be patient and observant in discerning the level of cultivation in a person.

Gauge by: Observation over a prolong period of time will reveal the level of cultivation in an individual.

 Incorruptibility

He is a wise man who does not grieve for the things which he has not,
but rejoices for those which he has.

– Epictetus

Incorruptibility is the measure of the individual's resistance to the effects of unwholesome vices and corruption.

Principle in Action

(**P**erson)

(**O**rganization)

(**W**hat Challenges)

(**E**xecution)

(**R**esults)

(**F**actors of Success/Failure)

(**U**nderstanding)

(**L**essons and insights)

The Aspects of Incorruptibility to Consider:

- o   The types of corrupting influences faced.
- o   The areas where these corrupting influences are aimed at.
- o   The manner in which these negative influences are handled and neutralized.
- o   The level of incorruptibility present and the critical factors supporting it.
- o   Changes in these vital factors will affect the individual's incorruptibility.

- o Other changes will also exert influences on incorruptibility.
- o (Reader's Insights)

The Essence: Incorruptibility bestows honor and inner peace.

Gauge by: Discover and take note of instances whereby the individual are being tempted by great rewards to discern the level of incorruptibility.

 Trustworthiness

"I'm not upset that you lied to me,
I'm upset that from now on I can't believe you."
– Friedrich Nietzsche

Trustworthiness is the individual's capacity for being "trustable" for the safeguard of delicate information or being "dependable" for being able to handle the tasks entrusted to him/her.

Principle in Action

(**P**erson)

(**O**rganization)

(**W**hat Challenges)

(**E**xecution)

(**R**esults)

(**F**actors of Success/Failure)

(**U**nderstanding)

(**L**essons and insights)

The Aspects of Trustworthiness to Consider:

- o The level of trustworthiness present.
- o The areas of trustworthiness being tested.

o The duration of observations.

o The accuracy of the observations.

o The manner in which assigned tasks are being completed by the individual.

o The ability of the individual to handle the assigned tasks.

o The end results of the tasks assigned to the individual.

o The manner and actions of the individual in facing success or failure in the assigned tasks.

o (Reader's Insights)

The Essence: Trustworthiness takes time and repeated shouldering of tasks to gauge.

Gauge by: Give the individual a series of tasks over a period of time, ranging from trivial to mediocre to challenging to gauge the levels of his/her capabilities and trustworthiness.

 # Changes

Change is the law of life;
and those who look only to the past or the present are certain to miss the future.
—*John F. Kennedy*

The changes discussed here are those that impact the blue ring of factors in the matrix.

Principle in Action

(**P**erson)

(**O**rganization)

(**W**hat Challenges)

(**E**xecution)

(**R**esults)

(**F**actors of Success/Failure)

(**U**nderstanding)

(**L**essons and insights)

The Aspects of Change to Consider:

- o The types of changes that appeared.
- o The areas of change in the factors in this blue ring of the matrix.
- o The speed of change.
- o The effects of the changes.
- o The constant observation and updating of one appraisal of the individual.
- o (Reader's Insights)

The Essence: Change changes everything. Efforts must be spent in keeping up to date on the critical developments that could change the current characteristics of the individual.

 # Execution

"Action expresses priorities."

– Mahatma Gandhi

Execution represents the whole range of skill sets that are put into action when the individual plans, prepares and acts to achieve his/her desired goals. Actions give shape and form to the dreams and goals of the individual.

Principle in Action

(**P**erson)

(**O**rganization)

(**W**hat Challenges)

(**E**xecution)

(**R**esults)

(**F**actors of Success/Failure)

(**U**nderstanding)

(**L**essons and insights)

The Aspects of Execution to Consider:

- o   The types of actions observed.
- o   The level of preparation that went into it.
- o   The objectives to be achieved and the results obtained.
- o   The individual's expectations and goals.
- o   The level of skill present/lacking shown.
- o   The signs of improvement/stagnation in the skills shown.
- o   The ability of the individual to handle random events that cropped up.
- o   The implications that the actions convey.
- o   The positive/negative factors supporting the action.
- o   The "style" of execution.
- o   The context, the situation and the people present during execution.
- o   (Reader's Insights)

The Essence: Learn to see the motives behind the actions of people.

 # Interaction

Difficulties are things that show what men are.

—Epictetus

Interaction encompasses the way in which the individual treats other people and living things as well. From the interactions, the cultivation and the hidden attributes of the individual are easily discerned.

Principle in Action

(**P**erson)

(**O**rganization)

(**W**hat Challenges)

(**E**xecution)

(**R**esults)

(**F**actors of Success/Failure)

(**U**nderstanding)

(**L**essons and insights)

<u>The Aspects of Interaction to Consider:</u>

- o The types of interaction observed.
- o The nature of the interactions.
- o The situation.
- o The location.
- o The timing.
- o The emotional state of the people involved.
- o The status of the people present/involved.
- o The state of the relationship (if any).
- o The cultural influences.
- o The purpose of the interaction.
- o (Reader's Insights)

The Essence: Discern the motives for the way people treat each other.

 Handling

Initiative is doing the right thing without being told.

– Victor Hugo

Handling represents the manner in which the individual treats non-living objects, his/her belongings and the belongings of others.

<u>Principle in Action</u>

(**P**erson)

(**O**rganization)

(**W**hat Challenges)

(**Execution**)

(**Results**)

(**Factors of Success/Failure**)

(**Understanding**)

(**Lessons and insights**)

The Aspects of Handling to Consider:

o   The level of respect accorded to his/her/others' belongings.
o   The manner in which the object is handled/managed.
o   The amount of care shown and the potential reason(s).
o   The level of utilization of the objects.
o   The state of organization of the objects.
o   The state of cleanliness of the objects (if applicable)
o   The way the objects are arranged/placed/kept.
o   (Reader's Insights)

The Essence: Reflect upon the attitudes and motivations of people from the way they treat objects.

Attitudes
Perspectives
Execution
态度
观点
执行
Goals
目标
Peace of Mind
安乐

Benefits
利
Liabilities
害

1 外事
1 志向
8 变
2 应变能力
1 性格
6 变化
2 原则
7 信用
3 意见
5 弱
4 强
价值观

6 清廉
4 胆略
3 接物
5 修养
2 待人

Resources
资源
Relinquish
弃

时
形
机

Timing
Forms
Opportunities

陶朱公商训第二则 能接纳

Tao Zhu Gong's Business Principle 2: The Ability to Handle People

THE SECOND BUSINESS PRINCIPLE— THE ABILITY TO HANDLE PEOPLE

When dealing with people, remember you are not dealing with creatures of logic, but creatures of emotion.

—Dale Carnegie

Ever since the first humans experienced the high survival rate bestowed by the power of groups, humans have being cooperating and corroborating with each other to rise up and grapple with all the challenges that are confronting the human race.

The ability of handling people is paramount to the survival and success of the individual, the company and society at large. The human mind is the ultimate success resource as all miraculous inventions and discoveries are being made through it alone. The ability to handle people, understand them, learn and innovate from them will produce endless wealth and success for the inquisitive and creative entrepreneur/enterprise.

To handle people well, we must first understand and establish the relationship of our inner attributes (see Chapter 1 TZG 1st Matrix) with the situations, the issues and the goals and the objectives. Next we must understand how our unique characteristics and skill sets function in the context of the relationship.

Being crystal clear about the nature of the relationship will enable the entrepreneur/enterprise to innovate/adapt to meet the needs and demands of the customers/stakeholders, hence dramatically increasing the potential of success.

This principle is especially pertinent for leaders and managers who will face the new generations of peers and subordinates in Gen Y and Gen Z.

The 13 Strategic Aspects

1. Understanding and Analysis
- *The knowledge of one's skills in relationship building.*

2. Acquisition of Information
- *The study of how great leaders and legendary entrepreneurs build relationships.*

3. The Battle Environment
- *The relationship forged.*

4. Topography of the Environment
- *The factors that affect the health of the relationship.*

5. Weakness and Strength
- *The discoveries of such in the context of relationship building skills.*

6. Commitment
- *The factors affecting the levels of commitment to the relationship by all parties.*

7. Strategic Planning
- *The strategies and tactics used for the advancement and maintenance of the relationship.*

8. Preparation
- *The costs of building a successful relationship.*

9. Competitive Advantage
- *The competitive advantage(s) or benefits bestowed by the relationship.*

10. The Maneuvers
- *The vital activities needed for building and maintaining the relationship.*

11. The Engagement
- *The actual interactions within the relationship.*

12. The Leadership
- *The win-win approach for the relationships.*

13. Change and Adaption
- *The influence of change on the nature of the relationship.*

The Matrix of Tao Zhu Gong's 2nd Business Principle (TZG 2nd Matrix)

The Components

The core matrix located in the centre is for the entrepreneur to use to gauge oneself and the person he/she is focusing on. The core matrix can even be used for analyzing companies to gauge their responses and reactions. By constructing an overall view picture of the client, the entrepreneur is better poised to prepare preemptively thereby increasing the chances of successfully meeting the goals in/from the relationship.

The red factors are explained in the sequence of attitudes, execution, peace of mind, liabilities, relinquish, opportunities, forms, timing, resources, benefits, goals and perspectives.

The Reading

Presented in this second matrix are the various factors that influence the relationships of people.

The second ring of factors focuses on what are the common factors or tools to aid in the handling of people, be it selling, negotiating, problem resolution in the context of the relationship etc.

These factors provide an arsenal of tools for the entrepreneur in tackling the tough challenges posed by people in his/her relationships.

 # Attitudes

Attitude is a little thing that makes a big difference.
— Winston S. Churchill

Attitude is the particular mindset that you project to the person, event, task that you are dealing with or observing. It influences how you perceive about the nature of the task, the viability etc. ultimately affecting your success potential.

Attitudes affect all aspects of the individual's life. Attitudes held by the people in the company will affect the performance and longevity of the company and its associates. Attitudes held by the general populace will influence and impact the overall health and prosperity of the societies.

Principle in Action

(**P**erson)

(**O**rganization)

(**W**hat Challenges)

(**E**xecution)

(**R**esults)

(**F**actors of Success/Failure)

(**U**nderstanding)

(**L**essons and insights)

The Essence: Maintain a constant level of respect and use the opportunities of any interaction to learn more about the other party. Knowing what to look for and why.

 # Execution

You can't cross the sea merely by standing and staring at the water.
—Rabindranath Tagore

Execution in this chapter means all the related actions pertaining to the interactions with the people. Human beings communicate via verbal communications, written words and non-verbal cues.

Messages and subtle meanings lay hidden behind every action and interaction. The person who can read these signals well would gain access to a whole new world of possibilities and opportunities.

Principle in Action

(**P**erson)

(**O**rganization)

(**W**hat Challenges)

(**E**xecution)

(**R**esults)

(**F**actors of Success/Failure)

(**U**nderstanding)

(**L**essons and insights)

The Essence: Balance effectiveness, efficiency, economy and expectations to achieve the optimal level of performance in the various situations you will face even in human interactions.

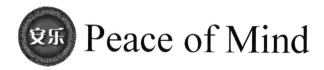 Peace of Mind

"Peace comes from within.
Do not seek it without."

—Gautama Buddha

Peace of Mind is the peaceful and stable state of mind. It is built on the perception that the issue will be meet and resolved successfully. In the business context, peace of mind also comes from the congruence of your principles, beliefs, values and the contributions of the company to society.

Peace of mind is vital for sustaining physical, mental and emotional health. Exposure to relentless worries and stress diminishes the quality of life that you lead while working or running your company.

Better to be well prepared for any potential crisis than to hope for miracles, for failing despite your best preparations leaves you with few regrets and emotional baggage to renew, reinvigorate and rise again.

Principle in Action

(**P**erson)

(**O**rganization)

(**W**hat Challenges)

(**E**xecution)

(**R**esults)

(**F**actors of Success/Failure)

(**U**nderstanding)

(**L**essons and insights)

The Essence: One of the many ways to enjoy peace of mind is to prepare in advance, prepare well and train for the various contingencies. The mental and emotional equilibrium will enable your mind to handle any changes calmly.

 Liabilities

"Mostly it is loss which teaches us about the worth of things."
—Arthur Schopenhauer

Liabilities in this chapter mean the potential/actual dangers, risks that may arise in the interactions between people. Liabilities are the real and potential damages that could materialize from simply engaging, disengaging or vacillating on the issues (the various intricacies and deals amongst people).

Since the beginning of time, unwholesome people existed and will continue to exist till the end of humanity. In the meantime, the ability to recognize the hidden dangers in human relationships will preempt many losses.

Principle in Action

(**P**erson)

(**O**rganization)

(**W**hat Challenges)

(**E**xecution)

(**R**esults)

(**F**actors of Success/Failure)

(**U**nderstanding)

(**L**essons and insights)

The Essence: Understand the nature of the various risks in your industry and other spheres of influence. Learn from the mistakes of others and from the wisdom of mentors (if any). This will minimize the losses suffered by you. Should the lesson be unavoidable, you have gained valuable experience.

(弃) Relinquish

The greatest loss of time is delay and expectation, which depend upon the future.
We let go the present, which we have in our power, and look forward to that which
depends upon chance, and so relinquish a certainty for an uncertainty.

– Seneca

Relinquish means conceding, yielding and in the extreme case discontinuation of the relationship or issue.

It embodies forsaking a pursuit due to the demands of strategic objectives (that have changed in time, making the pursuit impractical and unfeasible) whereby a better option appears or the current pursuit does not best serve one's new goals.

We do not have infinite resources and time to pursue every opportunity. There are real limits to our energies, capabilities and that of the organization.

Principle in Action

(**P**erson)

(**O**rganization)

(**W**hat Challenges)

(**E**xecution)

(**R**esults)

(**F**actors of Success/Failure)

(**U**nderstanding)

(**L**essons and insights)

The Essence: There are times to let go for a while. There are times to permanently let go. The essence lies in the wisdom to know when.

 # Opportunities

Small opportunities are often the beginning of great enterprises.

– Demosthenes

Opportunities in the context of handling human relationships and the various types of people, personalities and roles involved means actively and strategically seeking out the situations, events, information that could bestow advantages to your position and benefits to the firm (albeit in a legal and honest/right manner).

People change. Their characters, goals and objectives change. Hence for the business and formal relationships, the changes in the organization will create flux in the current relationships that the reader is in, windows of opportunity to grasp and make use of.

Successful people do not succeed alone. They cultivate and possess great networks of good quality people to support them in facing the trials and challenges in their quest for success.

Principle in Action

(**P**erson)

(**O**rganization)

(**W**hat Challenges)

(**E**xecution)

(**R**esults)

(**F**actors of Success/Failure)

(**U**nderstanding)

(**L**essons and insights)

The Essence: Ensure that the chance to advance or strengthen your position is really an opportunity instead of wishful thinking or erroneous perception and act accordingly.

 Forms

One of the most sincere forms of respect is actually listening to what another has to say.

– Bryant McGill

Forms (of the relationships) follow the function and phase that the relationship is undergoing. Function of the relationship is dictated by the goals of the organization.

Goals of the organization are dependent on the goals of its top management and leaders. Circumstances change, people change, goals and objectives are altered to adhere and adapt to the new conditions. Therefore it is inevitable that the form of the relationship will undergo some changes.

Forms are the styles, shapes and manifestations of the invisible workings. For example, you cannot actually see anger; you can only see its physical manifestations.

Principle in Action

(**P**erson)

(**O**rganization)

(**W**hat Challenges)

(**E**xecution)

(**R**esults)

(**F**actors of Success/Failure)

(**U**nderstanding)

(**L**essons and insights)

The Essence: The Taoists believe that the meaning of the visible is defined by the invisible. Hence this is the essence of discerning the true forms of things.

 # Timing

Observe due measure, for right timing is in all things the most important factor.

— Hesiod

Timing (in relationship) is built upon the concentration of preparation, the window of opportunity and decisive execution to bring forth success.

Timing in all things is eternally vital. Even in the realm of relationships, the factors of timing cannot be underestimated.

Every relationship has it ebbs and flows, phases and cycles. By understanding and capturing the appropriate windows of timing to say and do something to enhance the relationship, one can add value and be in the good books of those involved.

Principle in Action

(**P**erson)

(**O**rganization)

(**W**hat Challenges)

(**E**xecution)

(**R**esults)

(**F**actors of Success/Failure)

(**U**nderstanding)

(**L**essons and insights)

The Essence: Opportunities are events or potential events that exist for the duration till their conditions for victory are met. The art of timing is grasping what the conditions of victory are, when and how to best fulfill them.

 # Resources

All the resources we need are in the mind.

—Theodore Roosevelt

Resources (in the context of relationships) generally mean the assets (physical or non-physical) that can be deployed from the relationship to benefit all parties.

The reality of things is the ultimate force in the building of relationships. Should the results gained from working together exceed the results from working alone, then there is a basis for cooperation.

By making use of assets/resources/competitive advantages that your firm is lacking from cooperative and beneficial ventures, you open up new doors of opportunity and growth.

This segment focuses on how to use resources to develop, strengthen and maintain the relationship.

Principle in Action

(**P**erson)

(**O**rganization)

(**W**hat Challenges)

(**E**xecution)

(**R**esults)

(**F**actors of Success/Failure)

(**U**nderstanding)

(**L**essons and insights)

The Essence: Anything that you can use to advance and strengthen your position is a resource (adhere to Bai Gui's Matrix for reference and guidance).

 # Benefits

Whom did it benefit?

(Cui Bono Fuerit)

— Longinus Cassius

Benefits (in the context of relationships) represent the advantages that the relationship brings to the parties.

Benefits are derived from a strategic mindset and defined by the demands of the goals to be achieved. Benefits are the end results of harnessing opportunities successfully.

In the realm of business, no one would pursue and develop a "useless" relationship.

Principle in Action

(**P**erson)

(**O**rganization)

(**W**hat Challenges)

(**E**xecution)

(**R**esults)

(**F**actors of Success/Failure)

(**U**nderstanding)

(**L**essons and insights)

The Essence: Benefits are anything that can strengthen and advance you towards your desired goals. Benefits and liabilities are two sides of the same coin; conditions of success will determine if it is a benefit or liability.

 # Goals

Define your business goals clearly so that others can see them as you do.

— George F. Burns

Goals here encompass all the goals and objectives for the relationships that are established and those yet established.

Goals are the desired outcomes of the individual in the perception that attaining it will add significant value to his/her life.

One must be crystal clear on the reasons for establishing the relationship and the objectives to be met and the lifespan of the relationship etc.

Principle in Action

(**P**erson)

(**O**rganization)

(**W**hat Challenges)

(**E**xecution)

(**R**esults)

(**F**actors of Success/Failure)

(**U**nderstanding)

(**L**essons and insights)

The Essence: Clarity of purpose, the costs and the conditions for success are the vital components to be achieved.

观点 Perspectives

It is important to live each day with a positive perspective. It is not wise to pretend problems do not exist, but it is wise to look beyond the problem to the possibilities that are in it. When Goliath came against the Israelites, the soldiers all thought, 'He's so big, we can never kill him.' But David looked at the same giant and thought, 'He's so big, I can't miss him.'

– Dr. Dale E. Turner

Perspectives are the various angles of view that the individual can adopt to consider an issue, person, event or an object. Only by understanding the relationship from multiple angles could one get the 'big picture' view of things.

Your character determines what default 'settings" or lenses that you choose to view the challenge. It is imperative to gain as wide an exposure to ferret any inaccurate views or preconceptions, assumptions held regarding the challenge.

Once you have the accurate and working macro view, then you can gauge and access the impact of your actions on the relationship and the possible reactions.

Principle in Action

(**P**erson)

(**O**rganization)

(**W**hat Challenges)

(**E**xecution)

(**R**esults)

(**F**actors of Success/Failure)

(**U**nderstanding)

(**L**essons and insights)

The Essence: The actions of most people are determined by their strongest perspectives (shaped by constant use or simply a lack of desire to explore new ones), ensure that you explore your choice of perspectives before deciding.

Political Trends

政治

Competitor
对手

Product / Service
产品服务

Technological Trends
科技

Enterprise
企业

Social Trends
社会

顾客
Customer

排名
Position In Industry

经济
Economy

陶朱公商训第三则 能安业

Tao Zhu Gong's Business Principle 3: The Ability to Focus Stabilize, Prosper & Transform

THE THIRD BUSINESS PRINCIPLE—
THE ABILITY TO FOCUS, STABILIZE,
PROSPER AND TRANSFORM

The difference between a successful person and others is not a lack of strength,
not a lack of knowledge, but rather a lack of will.
—Vince Lombardi

Tao Zhu Gong meant the entrepreneur/enterprise must be able to achieve relative stability in order to succeed. To achieve stability, the entrepreneur/enterprise must first focus on achieving the basic business targets to survive, while working to create a stable enterprise in terms of human capital, financial capital and reserves, effective and efficient production of products/services and visionary management.

Once such relative stability is achieved, it will empower the entrepreneur/enterprise with the means to strive for prosperity via vying for a bigger market share or creating strong competitive advantages powered by research and innovation. After the enterprise has achieved success and prosperity, it is time to plan and transform to face the new trends and challenges that will come in the cycle of change and renewal.

This in essence is what the third business principle encompasses.

The 13 Strategic Aspects

1. Understanding and Analysis
- *The factors that could destroy the enterprise.*

2. Acquisition of Information
- *The histories of failed businesses, states and countries spanning the eras and boundaries.*

3. The Battle Environment
- *The overall business environment that the enterprise is operating in.*

4. Topography of the Environment
-   *The critical factors that are vital for the continued success of the enterprise.*

5. Weakness and Strength
-   *The augmentation of strengths and the elimination of weaknesses.*

6. Commitment
-   *The level of overall commitment marshaled for the implementation of the proposed plans.*

7. Strategic Planning
-   *The strategies and tactics used for sustaining success and facing new changes.*

8. Preparation
-   *The resources to marshal and to commit.*

9. Competitive Advantage
-   *The competitive advantage(s) to use in the ongoing processes of the enterprise.*

10. The Maneuvers
-   *The implementation and execution of planned activities.*

11. The Engagement
-   *The control and monitoring of the ongoing progress.*

12. The Leadership
-   *The moods and morale of the stakeholders during the phases of progress.*

13. Change and Adaption
-   *The influence of new change that impact the activities in progression.*

The Matrix of Tao Zhu Gong's 3rd Business Principle (TZG 3rd Matrix)

The Components

The core matrix is used to analyze the entrepreneur and the stakeholders.

The red factors are explained in the sequence of political trends, social trends, economy and lastly technological trends.

The blue ones are explained in the sequence of product/service, position in industry, customer and lastly competitor.

The Reading

The red factors represent the macro view and the blue factors represent the micro view of the sources of change impacting the enterprise constantly.

 # Political Trends

*One of the penalties for refusing to participate in politics is that
you end up being governed by your inferiors.*

—Plato

Political trends represent the direction that the government of the country, region, and area is headed.

Political trends encompass the goals, stance, direction and governmental styles of the political parties working in tandem.

Political stability via a principled, capable, fair and functioning government with effective business friendly policies provides the basis for businesses to prosper and thrive.

Principle in Action

(**P**erson)

(**O**rganization)

(**W**hat Challenges)

(**E**xecution)

(**R**esults)

(**F**actors of Success/Failure)

(**U**nderstanding)

(**L**essons and insights)

The Essence: Equilibrium and disequilibrium exist in an eternal cycle. Know your governments to prosper during stability and to protect during chaotic conditions.

 Social Trends

A society grows great when old men plant trees in whose shade they know they shall never sit.

– Greek proverb

Social trends mean are the various trends in the demographics of the area, country or region.

People are the bedrock of society. Any changes in a significant portion of the population will ripple out to influence the entire society at large.

The changes brought by social trends mold the demands/perceptions of the current products/ services offered by companies. The company must be up to date with these trends to survive by staying relevant and prosper by catering to the new demands.

Principle in Action

(**P**erson)

(**O**rganization)

(**W**hat Challenges)

(**E**xecution)

(**R**esults)

(**F**actors of Success/Failure)

(**U**nderstanding)

(**L**essons and insights)

The Essence: People are the water that can float or sink a boat (your industry). Understanding social trends is akin to understanding how water will flow in the given conditions.

 Economy

People want economy and they will pay any price to get it.

—Lee Iacocca

Economy here represents the trends that are present in the economy of the country or region. The trends are reflective of the business cycles and fluctuations that are inherent in any economy.

Due to the interconnectedness of today's world via trade and investment flows, it is relatively easy for financial shocks to affect and influence a large portion of the world economy as evidenced by the financial crisis of 2009.

These cycles repeat themselves as surely as the seasonal changes. Hence one must be prepared for the good times and lean times. To think otherwise and believe in any talk of "new" economic models is to reap harvests of pain when the economy underperforms or teeters on the brink of collapse.

Principle in Action

(**P**erson)

(**O**rganization)

(**W**hat Challenges)

(**E**xecution)

(**R**esults)

(**F**actors of Success/Failure)

(**U**nderstanding)

(**L**essons and insights)

The Essence: Prepare to meet the conditions for success or survival in times of austerity and prosperity.

科技 Technological Trends

Any sufficiently advanced technology is indistinguishable from magic.
—Arthur C. Clarke

Technological advancements advance human civilization. From the telegram to the telephone and the wireless communication of the modern era, we are still in the midst of new technological advancements.

Technological trends are the prevailing technological advancements that are being used._The opportunities manifest when mass adoption of any technology on a massive scale occurs, bringing inevitable changes to the society and businesses.

Vast fortunes can be made at this cusp of change.

Principle in Action

(**P**erson)

(**O**rganization)

(**W**hat Challenges)

(**E**xecution)

(**R**esults)

(**F**actors of Success/Failure)

(**U**nderstanding)

(**L**essons and insights)

The Essence: Innovations are relentless, unstoppable, and inevitable bringing forth lasting changes to your industry. Be prepared or be left behind.

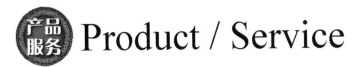 # Product / Service

Junk is the ultimate merchandise.
The junk merchant does not sell his product to the consumer; he sells the consumer to the product.
He does not improve and simplify his merchandise; he degrades and simplifies the client.

—William Seward Burroughs

Product/Service is the final good that the company manufactures/creates to earn its revenue. The focus here is the relevance of your products/services in relation to the ever-changing consumer tastes and your competitors' advancements.

Your products/services must be relevant and functional (refer to industry norms and conventions) and value adding. Customers will realize in a matter of time.

In short, do not produce products/services of little worth.

Principle in Action

(**P**erson)

(**O**rganization)

(**W**hat Challenges)

(**E**xecution)

(**R**esults)

(**F**actors of Success/Failure)

(**U**nderstanding)

(**L**essons and insights)

The Essence: Do not produce or sell mediocre product(s)/service(s), it is akin to committing company hara kiri.

Position In Industry

Do not pursue what is illusory - property and position all that is gained at the expense of your nerves decade after decade and can be confiscated in one fell night. Live with a steady superiority over life - don't be afraid of misfortune, and do not yearn after happiness it is after all, all the same the bitter doesn't last forever, and the sweet never fills the cup to overflowing.

—Alexander Solzhenitsyn

Position in Industry represents the rank of the company in its industry. It is based upon the various surveys and tests that your company is subjected and reviewed to come to a ranking.

You can use this information as a baseline for you to compare, discover weaknesses and build up your competencies.

Strengths and weaknesses are interchangeable and non-permanent. They exist in flux in relation to each other and the current competitive environment in which the company operates.

Depending on the metrics of the tests, surveys and studies conducted, the findings/rankings paint a picture that are based on the factors measured and/or may not be indicative of the competencies of the whole company in relation to other competitors.

Understanding the methodologies used and how your company is ranked in relation to others will produce insights into areas of improvements. Hence when the next wave of change comes, you are better poised for seizing the opportunities in the upheaval that ensued.

Principle in Action

(**P**erson)

(**O**rganization)

(**W**hat Challenges)

(**E**xecution)

(**R**esults)

(**F**actors of Success/Failure)

(**U**nderstanding)

(**L**essons and insights)

The Essence: Understand "where", "why" and "how" you are ranked in your niche. Then you can commence to improve via "what" to climb the rankings.

 # Customer

It is not the employer who pays the wages. Employers only handle the money.

It is the customer who pays the wages.

—Henry Ford

In chapter 2, we learnt about the general factors in the handling of people. In business, customers are the people who purchase the goods and services provided by companies, hence they are one of the core groups of people that the firm must learn to handle well.

To handle customers, the entrepreneur/enterprise must first know them well, their needs and the value of your products/services to them.

Serious time and effort must be spent learning about customers, for they are the water that ship sails on. Like the oceans, rivers and lakes, they have their ebbs and flows.

<u>Principle in Action</u>

(**P**erson)

(**O**rganization)

(**W**hat Challenges)

(**E**xecution)

(**R**esults)

(**F**actors of Success/Failure)

(**U**nderstanding)

(**L**essons and insights)

The Essence: Customers are like orchards. Planning, care and resources are required to setup and maintain a successful orchard.

 Competitor

The biggest things are always the easiest to do because there is no competition.

–William Van Horne

A competitor can be defined as a firm/person who is in competition with the entrepreneur/enterprise for the same prize (same market share in a common area etc.). Yet the difference between partners, customers and competitors is separated by a fine line.

Simply put, if the other firm/party is in the same industry, serving the same customer base with similar products/services, then it is a competitor.

Your competitors and how well you fare against them is the testament and true reflection of your skills and capabilities.

Principle in Action

(**P**erson)

(**O**rganization)

(**W**hat Challenges)

(**E**xecution)

(**R**esults)

(**F**actors of Success/Failure)

(**U**nderstanding)

(**L**essons and insights)

The Essence: Ally and/or competitor, the roles are determined by intent; whether they aid in your success or failure depends on how your deal with them.

Leadership

领导

Excellence

卓越

Effectiveness

奏效

People

人事

Enterprise

企业

Production / Service

产品
服务

Economy

经济

Finances

财务

Efficiency

高效

陶朱公商训第四则　能整顿

Tao Zhu Gong's Business Principle 4: The Ability to Be Organized

THE FOURTH BUSINESS PRINCIPLE—
THE ABILITY TO BE ORGANIZED

The secret of success in life is for a man to be ready for his opportunity when it comes.
—Benjamin Disraeli

Great companies have mastered coordination within their organizational structures to produce the ability to adapt and align their resources to rise to the challenges.

Through being principled, flexible in implementation and execution, effective in producing desired results, efficient in the use of resources and clear in the objectives to achieve, masterful coordination will bring great order and immense value to the entrepreneur/enterprise.

In the competitive business arenas throughout the world, disorganized entrepreneurs/enterprises are being weakened, wiped out or assimilated by better organized competitors

The 13 Strategic Aspects

1. Understanding and Analysis
   * *The knowledge of what to be focused and acted upon.*

2. Acquisition of Information
   * *The performance of the enterprise in relation to others.*

3. The Battle Environment
   * *The inner world of the enterprise.*

4. Topography of the Environment
   * *The factors that weaken or restrict the effectiveness and success potential.*

5. Weakness and Strength
   * *The discovery in the context of organization to craft a great enterprise.*

6. Commitment
   * *The entrepreneur and stake holders' wills.*

7. Strategic Planning
- *The areas and aspects to refine for better performances.*

8. Preparation
- *The requirements for the tasks.*

9. Competitive Advantage
- *The competitive advantage(s) or benefits to be strengthened/gained.*

10. The Maneuvers
- *The implementation of the plans.*

11. The Engagement
- *The control of the progression.*

12. The Leadership
- *The morale of the enterprise throughout the process.*

13. Change and Adaption
- *The performance of the new changes in relation to the challenges met and conquered.*

The Matrix of Tao Zhu Gong's 4th Business Principle (TZG 4th Matrix)

The Components

The core matrix is used in the context of analyzing the enterprise as a human. As enterprises do take on the characteristics and styles of their leaders.

The red factors are explained in the sequence of leadership, production/service, finances and people.

The blue ones are explained in the sequence of effectiveness, efficiency, economy and excellence.

The Reading

The fourth matrix showcases the vital red factors affecting the "stability" of the enterprise in the face of the sources of change from the 3rd matrix. The blue factors are the guidelines for gauging the actions taken for stabilizing and organizing the enterprise.

 # Enterprise

A man who does not plan long ahead will find trouble right at his door.

—Confucius

Enterprise (in this context) means the whole enterprise, the whole set of goals, resources, strategic focus, skills, strengths and weaknesses that the firm brings to the competitive arena.

Understand that the effects of an organization do impact society; some more forcibly while others subtly. The strength of the firm's influence depends on the value of its products/services and the elasticity of demand and supply.

The Essence: An enterprise can be viewed as a human being, with changing phases of beliefs, principles and characteristics with each new leader/top management.

 # Leadership

"I have three precious things which I hold fast and prize. The first is gentleness; the second is frugality; the third is humility, which keeps me from putting myself before others. Be gentle and you can be bold; be frugal and you can be liberal; avoid putting yourself before others and you can become a leader among men."

— Lao Tzu

Leadership encompasses the whole leadership set of skills being brought in play at the helm of the company. Leadership (visible acts of leadership) in this chapter deals with the issues of leading the company whereas in chapter 11, it is explored in greater detail.

The importance of leaders in company cannot be underestimated, the effects of leadership is far reaching and possess significant impact on the lives of the people under its mantle and leaders hold the fate of the company.

To prosperity, to stagnation or to ruin, be it in firms, political parties or government, people have to choose one of the three paths via their of choice of leaders. Choose wisely.

Principle in Action

(**P**erson)

(**O**rganization)

(**W**hat Challenges)

(**E**xecution)

(**R**esults)

(**F**actors of Success/Failure)

(**U**nderstanding)

(**L**essons and insights)

The Essence: Weak or ineffective leadership is toxic to self, company or society. Nothing good can come out of weak leadership.

 # Production / Service

Quality in a product or service is not what the supplier puts in. It is what the customer gets out and is willing to pay for. A product is not quality because it is hard to make and costs a lot of money, as manufacturers typically believe. This is incompetence. Customers pay only for what is of use to them and gives them value. Nothing else constitutes quality.

—*Peter Drucker*

Production/Service means the process of making the products or providing the services that the company sells. This factor deals with the capability of the company to produce good quality products/services.

Should any event compromises the productions/services, the firm will be impacted and impaired. With prolonged impairment in this factor comes ruin and bankruptcy.

For no firm can withstand prolonged production/service problems without suffering dire consequences.

Principle in Action

(**P**erson)

(**O**rganization)

(**W**hat Challenges)

(**E**xecution)

(**R**esults)

(**F**actors of Success/Failure)

(**U**nderstanding)

(**L**essons and insights)

The Essence: Balance between making/selling good products with earning health profits.

 # Finances

> *"Rule No. 1: Never lose money.*
> *Rule No. 2: Never forget Rule No. 1."*
>
> —*Warren Buffett*

Finances encompass the whole sphere of the company financial workings.

It is akin to the blood and circulatory system of the human body. Should anything happen to the volume of blood flowing/present in the body, then dire and life threatening consequences are bound to manifest.

Finances are the circulatory system and cash flows are the lifeblood of the enterprise.

Principle in Action

(**P**erson)

(**O**rganization)

(**W**hat Challenges)

(**E**xecution)

(**R**esults)

(**F**actors of Success/Failure)

(**U**nderstanding)

(**L**essons and insights)

The Essence: Many an empire and company comes to ruin via the instability in its finances.

 # People

> *"In individuals, insanity is rare;*
> *but in groups, parties, nations and epochs,*
> *it is the rule."*
>
> *—Friedrich Nietzsche*

People mentioned in this factor represent the whole spectrum of people working in the firm and whether their skills and capabilities are being maximized for the success of the firm.

The keyword is unity and a unified company can produce wonders._People and people alone drive and propel your company towards success or ruin.

Principle in Action

(**P**erson)

(**O**rganization)

(**W**hat Challenges)

(**E**xecution)

(**R**esults)

(**F**actors of Success/Failure)

(**U**nderstanding)

(**L**essons and insights)

The Essence: People are the ultimate resource. Learn to handle and use them well.

 # Effectiveness

> *Practical wisdom is only to be learned in the school of experience.*
> *Precepts and instruction are useful so far as they go, but, without the discipline of real life,*
> *they remain of the nature of theory only.*
>
> —*Samuel Smiles*

Effectiveness is the measure of the means and the results in the resolution of a challenge. It is the measure of the effects of the actions taken to meet a challenge and the completeness of the victory.

Principle in Action

(**P**erson)

(**O**rganization)

(**W**hat Challenges)

(**E**xecution)

(**R**esults)

(**F**actors of Success/Failure)

(**U**nderstanding)

(**L**essons and insights)

The Essence: The basic measure of effectiveness is objectives being accomplished.

 Efficiency

There is nothing so useless as doing efficiently that which should not be done at all.

—Peter Drucker

Efficiency is the measure of the utilization of resources consumed in the achievement of an objective. Improving efficiency means using fewer resources to achieve comparable results under the same situation/challenge/problem.

For humans, there is a limit to the amount of work done, the optimal balance between work-life.

Principle in Action

(**P**erson)

(**O**rganization)

(**W**hat Challenges)

(**E**xecution)

(**R**esults)

(**F**actors of Success/Failure)

(**U**nderstanding)

(**L**essons and insights)

The Essence: Objectives are fulfilled with the optimal use of resources.

 Economy

Spare no expense to make everything as economical as possible.
—Samuel Goldwyn

Economy is measure of the quality of the resources used in achieving the same objective. It is the use of cheaper alternatives to achieve similar or comparable results.

Principle in Action

(**P**erson)

(**O**rganization)

(**W**hat Challenges)

(**E**xecution)

(**R**esults)

(**F**actors of Success/Failure)

(**U**nderstanding)

(**L**essons and insights)

The Essence: Objectives are accomplished with cheaper alternatives.

 # Excellence

The noblest search is the search for excellence.

—Lyndon B. Johnson

Excellence is the measure of the achieved results exceeding the initial expectations.

The standards of excellence are many and can be confusing. To clarify, ask yourself whose standards matters and why.

Principle in Action

(**P**erson)

(**O**rganization)

(**W**hat Challenges)

(**E**xecution)

(**R**esults)

(**F**actors of Success/Failure)

(**U**nderstanding)

(**L**essons and insights)

The Essence: Effectiveness, efficiency and economy combined to produce results that exceed expectations.

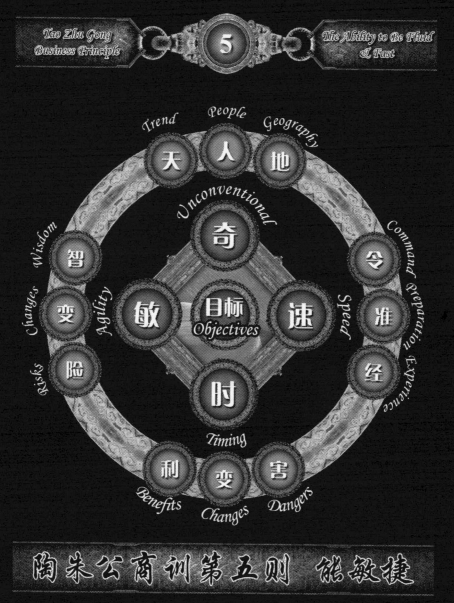

陶朱公商训第五则 能敏捷

Tao Zhu Gong's Business Principle 5: The Ability to Be Fluid & Fast

The Fifth Business Principle—The Ability to be Fluid and Fast

Perception is strong and sight weak. In strategy, it is important to see distant things as if they were close and to take a distanced view of close things.

—Miyamoto Musashi

The entrepreneur/enterprise fortified with the powerful benefits of an internally organized and financially healthy company will have at his/her disposal, a wide array of powerful strategic options for growing the company in its eternal quest for opportunities to grow and prosper.

Before committing to pursuing opportunities, one must first know/discern the relevance, the advantages bestowed, the costs of failure and the various positive and negative subtleties that could arise from acquiring the targeted opportunity.

The fifth principle deals with the various strategic considerations for the entrepreneur/enterprise in choosing and acquiring opportunities.

The 13 Strategic Aspects

1. Understanding and Analysis
- *The choice of strategies, tactics and execution in the midst of intense competition.*

2. Acquisition of Information
- *The accurate overview of the whole dynamic situation.*

3. The Battle Environment
- *The dynamic environments that the enterprise operates and competes in.*

4. Topography of the Environment
- *The areas/factors that offer new growth or advantages.*

5. Weakness and Strength
- *The discoveries made in the context of adapting to change successfully.*

6. Commitment
- *The courage and will of the entrepreneur and stakeholders in facing uncertainty and fierce competition.*

7. Strategic Planning
- *The strategies and tactics used for neutralizing the competitors' competitive advantages.*

8. Preparation
- *The costs of execution of the strategies and tactics.*

9. Competitive Advantage
- *The alignment of the enterprise's competitive advantages at the weaknesses of the competitors.*

10. The Maneuvers
- *The skillful execution of the strategies and tactics.*

11. The Engagement
- *The control of the initiatives in the engagement with the competitors.*

12. The Leadership
- *The morale of the stakeholders in the phases of battle.*

13. Change and Adaption
- *The counter reactions of the competitors.*

The Matrix of Tao Zhu Gong's 5th Business Principle (TZG 5th Matrix)

The Components

The core of the fifth matrix are the objectives of the enterprise to be achieved in the business ventures.

The red factors are explained in the sequence of unconventional (with trend, people and geography), speed (with command, preparation and experience), timing (with benefits, changes and dangers) and agility (with wisdom, changes and risks).

The Reading

The red strategic factors are guided by the purple objective while being supported by the blue factors of critical considerations.

 # Objectives

Failure comes only when we forget our ideals and objectives and principles.
                                                    —Jawaharal Nehru

Objectives are the bridging targets that must be achieved to attain success. In this case, the overall strategy of the enterprise must be in congruence with its goals, available resources and the general business terrain and competitors that lie within.

Change is the universal constant that must be monitored and adapted to. Hence firms must be able to adapt their strategies and objectives. For these are man-targets and must be reexamined in light of new developments.

Principle in Action

(**Person**)

(**Organization**)

(**What** Challenges)

(**Execution**)

(**Results**)

(**Factors** of Success/Failure)

(**Understanding**)

(**Lessons** and insights)

The Essence: Set objectives that further and advance your position.

Unconventional

For nonconformity the world whips you with its displeasure.
—Ralph Waldo Emerson

Unconventional means the new ways of thinking, analysis, execution and implementation that lead to success over tough challenges and problems.

What was unconventional in the past and successful would be emulated and copied by others hence becoming the new convention in dealing with similar problems and challenges. To be unconventional, know the norms and seek out new innovative ways to achieve success.

Caution is advised before rocking the boat, for some norms and conventions are established for safety reasons. Understand the history of these norms will allow you insights into where and how you can create new safe methods/products/services without endangering the lives of others.

The ability to come up with unconventional approaches sources from the difference in vision and focus of the entrepreneur.

Principle in Action

(**P**erson)

(**O**rganization)

(**W**hat Challenges)

(**E**xecution)

(**R**esults)

(**F**actors of Success/Failure)

(**U**nderstanding)

(**L**essons and insights)

The Essence: The unforeseen and the unpredictable. Only by training in advance to face such threats can you be calm and disciplined to react proportionately.

 # Trends

I find the great thing in this world is, not so much where we stand, as in what direction we are moving.

—Johann von Goethe

Trend (in accordance to unconventional) means the general direction of the event, people and issue. Trends can also encompass any significant directions in the company's spheres of activities and the STEP (Social, Technological, Economical, Political) factors.

To operate without knowing the trends that are happening and the possible scenarios of success/failure is to expose yourself needlessly to unnecessary risks.

Even when faced with the trends, different entrepreneurs will interpret the same trends differently and arrive at different conclusions. Hence to become unconventional, it is wise to know what are the most of the businesses thinking and expecting (conventional) and act innovatively.

Principle in Action

(**P**erson)

(**O**rganization)

(**W**hat Challenges)

(**E**xecution)

(**R**esults)

(**F**actors of Success/Failure)

(**U**nderstanding)

(**L**essons and insights)

The Essence: Timing, the weather and unexpected events that strike out of the blue. The one who can constantly steer events to one's advantage will be the victor.

 People

I need not fear my enemies because the most they can do is attack me. I need not fear my friends because the most they can do is betray me. But I have much to fear from people who are indifferent.

—*Assyrian Proverb*

People (in accordance to unconventional) in this factor mean the changes that are being manifested in them and how the whole dynamics of things could and would be changed.

The people is like the ocean that floats your ship (enterprise), you as the captain must know how to read the weather and sea conditions to ensure that your ship can navigate successfully.

Principle in Action

(**P**erson)

(**O**rganization)

(**W**hat Challenges)

(**E**xecution)

(**R**esults)

(**F**actors of Success/Failure)

(**U**nderstanding)

(**L**essons and insights)

The Essence: Any chaos or disruptions in the human aspects will offer a host of opportunities to seize and utilize.

⊞ Geography

He who knows the surface of the earth and the topography of a country only through the examination of maps...is like a man who learns the opera of Meyerbeer or Rossini by reading only reviews in the newspapers. The brush of landscape artists Lorrain, Ruysdael, or Calame can reproduce on canvas the sun's ray, the coolness of the heavens, the green of the fields, the majesty of the mountains... but what can never be stolen from Nature is that vivid impression that she alone can and knows how to impart--the music of the birds, the movement of the trees, the aroma peculiar to the place--the inexplicable something the traveler feels that cannot be defined and which seems to awaken in him distant memories of happy days, sorrows and joys gone by, never to return!

– Dr. Jose P. Rizal

Geography (in accordance to unconventional) is the topography of the firm and markets. There are the invisible mental and emotional topographies of the customers and competitors to consider. Various geographical aspects provide unique challenges and opportunities for the entrepreneurs to make use of.

Principle in Action

(**P**erson)

(**O**rganization)

(**W**hat Challenges)

(**E**xecution)

(**R**esults)

(**F**actors of Success/Failure)

(**U**nderstanding)

(**L**essons and insights)

The Essence: The one who can optimize and assimilate the advantages offered by the physical terrain and the invisible geography (the inner worlds of the opponents, allies etc.) of the battlegrounds will be successful.

 # Speed

Delay always breeds danger and to protract a great design is often to ruin it.

– Miguel de Cervantes

Speed is the rate at which actions are being executed to achieve the objectives. It is the time taken to achieve/complete an action.

Businesses need to grow to prosper and to fulfil its responsibilities to its people and society at large. Understand that opportunities do not exist for long. Thus the dire consequences of businesses missing out on too many opportunities will result in financial problems and ultimately bankruptcy.

Speed and prior preparations are the vital basics in securing opportunities.

Principle in Action

(**P**erson)

(**O**rganization)

(**W**hat Challenges)

(**E**xecution)

(**R**esults)

(**F**actors of Success/Failure)

(**U**nderstanding)

(**L**essons and insights)

The Essence: A delicate balance between speed, preparations and the ever-shrinking windows of opportunity.

# Command

What you cannot enforce, do not command.

— *Sophocles*

Command (in accordance to speed) represents the orders of the top management or superior. Commands must be clear and focused.

To be an effective leader, you cannot micromanage everything. Even if it is possible, the employees will suffer from low morale and productivity. It is better to announce your visions and goals, and delegate appropriate levels of authority to your subordinates and let them unleash their creativity and innovation to achieve your goals. Still it is vital to keep the lines of communication open, should your subordinates seek your counsel.

To seize the opportunity quickly, the entrepreneur and the company must be able to move fast and effectively. Only by having good relations between the leaders and employees could the company move fast.

Principle in Action

(**P**erson)

(**O**rganization)

(**W**hat Challenges)

(**E**xecution)

(**R**esults)

(**F**actors of Success/Failure)

(**U**nderstanding)

(**L**essons and insights)

The Essence: Clarity of commands, followed by clean execution of orders.

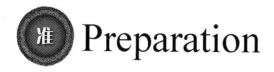 Preparation

Dig the well before you are thirsty.

—Chinese Proverb

Preparation (in accordance to speed) is the range of activities that aims at achieving the accumulation of resources, the analysis of all aspects of the tasks, the planning and potential execution to successfully achieve the targets and goals of the company.

To prepare is to ready and marshal all the relevant materials/resources to the fulfilment of the goals. For those who found that success comes relatively easy, they must have fulfilled in advance the prerequisites of their challenges.

Time is needed for preparations; in order to be fast, one must have the vision to plan in advance and accordingly.

No lasting success comes without proper prior preparations.

Principle in Action

(**P**erson)

(**O**rganization)

(**W**hat Challenges)

(**E**xecution)

(**R**esults)

(**F**actors of Success/Failure)

(**U**nderstanding)

(**L**essons and insights)

The Essence: Prepare well for success or prepare to fail.

 # Experience

By three methods we may learn wisdom.
First, by reflection, which is noblest.
Second, by imitation, which is easiest.
Third by experience, which is the bitterest.

— *Confucius*

Experience (in accordance to speed) is the accumulation of all exposures and encounters of the individual and forged into insights of value by the individual's fire of wisdom. As wisdom grows within the individual, it offers new powerful perspectives to review past encounters thus increasing your mastery over self.

The entrepreneur must gain a level of experience and mastery before moving fast. When in doubt, move cautiously and maintain strict control over one's emotions.

Principle in Action

(**P**erson)

(**O**rganization)

(**W**hat Challenges)

(**E**xecution)

(**R**esults)

(**F**actors of Success/Failure)

(**U**nderstanding)

(**L**essons and insights)

The Essence: Learn and assimilate from the experiences of others.

 # Timing

Observe due measure, for right timing is in all things the most important factor.

—Hesiod

Timing in this factor deals with the choice of the optimal time to launch an action. Timing must match strategic objectives, the preparations and flexible implementation in order to be effective.

The potential risks of the actions to be taken must be considered before in advance, only then when the opportunity arises can one immediately seize it.

Principle in Action

(**P**erson)

(**O**rganization)

(**W**hat Challenges)

(**E**xecution)

(**R**esults)

(**F**actors of Success/Failure)

(**U**nderstanding)

(**L**essons and insights)

The Essence: Timing is the seizing of opportunities at the right time by decisive actions backed by planning and preparation.

 # Benefits

Every advantage in the past is judged in the light of the final issue.
—Demosthenes

Benefits (in accordance to timing) are the advantages to be gained from choosing the particular time window for action.

Only in-depth prior analysis of the macro and micro overall situation can give you the insights to see where the potential benefits are in the choice of timing.

Principle in Action

(**P**erson)

(**O**rganization)

(**W**hat Challenges)

(**E**xecution)

(**R**esults)

(**F**actors of Success/Failure)

(**U**nderstanding)

(**L**essons and insights)

The Essence: In the flux of change, opportunities can become liabilities. Be aware of the factors that aid in the transformation.

 Changes

Everything changes, nothing remains without change.

– Buddha

Changes (in accordance to timing) represent the transformations that are manifested with the passage of time and the various interactions of all the factors, creating a flux of disorder and chaos. In times of chaos, only those who are prepared will be unaffected and are in a position to benefit from it.

Principle in Action

(**P**erson)

(**O**rganization)

(**W**hat Challenges)

(**E**xecution)

(**R**esults)

(**F**actors of Success/Failure)

(**U**nderstanding)

(**L**essons and insights)

The Essence: Time changes everything. Hence everything must change with time.

 # Dangers

He who learns but does not think, is lost! He who thinks but does not learn is in great danger.

—Confucius

Dangers (in accordance to timing) are the potential dangerous situations that could arise.

As an entrepreneur, one must be on guard against many risks and dangers; it is within reason to prepare for the foreseeable ones.

For those unexpected crises, only the skills and preparations made in time of peace can tide you over and provide the rare commodity of confidence so lacking in dangerous times.

Principle in Action

(**P**erson)

(**O**rganization)

(**W**hat Challenges)

(**E**xecution)

(**R**esults)

(**F**actors of Success/Failure)

(**U**nderstanding)

(**L**essons and insights)

The Essence: In the flux of change, dangers can become opportunities. Be aware of the factors that aid in the transformation.

 # Agility

Our biggest strategic risk is not being able to change ahead of it, we are bound by internal process and decision-making ... that leads us to believe we can take long periods of time to do things – that's not the world we live in today. We have got to become more strategically agile in everything from education to training.

—Mark Walsh

Agility is the ability to maneuver to positions of advantages and to avoid dangers.

It is particularly vital during times of great flux, those who are prepared have the ability to be agile and adapt to the changing conditions of the chaotic situations.

The agility to change one's planned course of action to accommodate new developments will prevent one from wasting precious resources in pursuit of futile targets (rendered futile by change).

Agility must be executed in accordance to the company's overarching imperatives to gain strategic advantage in a competitive environment.

Principle in Action

(**P**erson)

(**O**rganization)

(**W**hat Challenges)

(**E**xecution)

(**R**esults)

(**F**actors of Success/Failure)

(**U**nderstanding)

(**L**essons and insights)

The Essence: Agility is the ability to adjust one's position to adapt to the changing conditions of success.

 # Wisdom

Not by age but by capacity is wisdom acquired.

—*Titus Maccius Plautus*

Wisdom (in accordance with agility) and the experience to know the right things to focus on, the appropriate actions to take at the appropriate time are vital in handling the flux and confusion generated by big changes during the executional phase of the plans.

Entrepreneurs must be observant and keenly aware of the changes that are happening and they must have the will and skills to turn any negative events into positive foundations for growth.

Negative events are plenty in the realms of business, the entrepreneur who can use these negative events as fuel for growth will rise and prosper over those who cannot.

Principle in Action

(**P**erson)

(**O**rganization)

(**W**hat Challenges)

(**E**xecution)

(**R**esults)

(**F**actors of Success/Failure)

(**U**nderstanding)

(**L**essons and insights)

The Essence: Know what is changing and how to act accordingly.

 # Changes

There is a time for some things, and a time for all things
a time for great things, and a time for small things.

—Miguel de Cervantes

The changes (in accordance to timing) here are the types of changes that can occur during the action phase of a business campaign. The focus here is the strengthening of the competitive spirit in oneself and others while the changes within the change are dealt in greater detail in Chapter 10.

By possessing a strong competitive spirit will empower the entrepreneur and the enterprise to be excited by the prospects of change. With such positive empowering mindset, the company is poised to embrace the changes and grow without fear holding it back.

Principle in Action

(**P**erson)

(**O**rganization)

(**W**hat Challenges)

(**E**xecution)

(**R**esults)

(**F**actors of Success/Failure)

(**U**nderstanding)

(**L**essons and insights)

The Essence: Plan in advance to minimize the negative consequences.

 # Risks

We must have the courage to bet on our ideas, to take the calculated risk, and to act.
Everyday living requires courage if life is to be effective and bring happiness.

—Maxwell Maltz

Risk (in accordance to agility) represents the potential dangers posed by the culmination of various damaging factors should the new plans and moves be executed poorly.

There is always an element of risk of failure even in the best prepared campaign; it is up to the people to handle the various issues and challenges that could potentially crop up.

Hence the entrepreneur who values and develops his/her talents has a strong safety net to rely on.

Principle in Action

(**P**erson)

(**O**rganization)

(**W**hat Challenges)

(**E**xecution)

(**R**esults)

(**F**actors of Success/Failure)

(**U**nderstanding)

(**L**essons and insights)

The Essence: Know yourself, your goals, your objectives, your overall capabilities and the situation or phases you are in. Only then can you pierce the vague veil of swirling possibilities.

Credit Worthiness 信誉

Discipline & Control 掌握

Worst Case Scenario 最坏打算

State of Finance 财务现状

Reputation 名誉

Respect 敬重

工商业常态 Industry Norms

勤备 Diligence

陶朱公商训第六则 能讨账

Tao Zhu Gong's Business Principle 6: The Ability to Receive Compensation

THE SIXTH BUSINESS PRINCIPLE—
THE ABILITY TO RECEIVE COMPENSATION

It is not the employer who pays the wages. He only handles the money.
It is the customers, product (and services) that pay the wages.

—Henry Ford

In the Chinese traditional medicine and martial arts, the "*qi*" is the life force of the body. *Qi* circulates around the body energizing the various organs and tissues. When the *qi* is weakened and restricted, areas with weak/limited *qi* begin to deteriorate. It is of utmost importance to sustain and strengthen the *qi* for great health and longevity.

In a similar fashion, the financial health (overall qi) in the company (body) will determine if the business entity will be healthy and resilient enough to fend off strategic actions from its competitors and face the relentless challenges in the constantly changing business environment.

Death/bankruptcy awaits those entrepreneurs/enterprises that ignored the physical/financial health of their bodies/businesses.

The sixth principle examines the various hard hitting factors that could immediately threaten the financial health of the enterprises.

The 13 Strategic Aspects

1. Understanding and Analysis
- *The importance and developing the abilities to build strong financial foundations.*

2. Acquisition of Information
- *The histories of failed businesses and states due to financial weaknesses.*

3. The Battle Environment
- *The cash flows, financial reserves and assets of the enterprise.*

4. Topography of the Environment
- *The factors that affect the financial health of the enterprise.*

5. Weakness and Strength
- *The discoveries in any profit centers and in the cost control measures.*

6. Commitment
- *The entrepreneur and the stakeholders' attitudes towards the painful cost cutting measures.*

7. Strategic Planning
- *The strategies and tactics for boosting profits, cutting costs and investing the reserves.*

8. Preparation
- *The resources to commit.*

9. Competitive Advantage
- *The talents/advantages available for deployment in the realm of finances.*

10. The Maneuvers
- *The careful and deliberate implementation.*

11. The Engagement
- *The evaluation of the results achieved.*

12. The Leadership
- *The morale of the stakeholders in the different phases of the implementation.*

13. Change and Adaption
- *The utilization of the cost savings and financial benefits gained.*

The Matrix of Tao Zhu Gong's 6th Business Principle (TZG 6th Matrix)

The Components

The core of the sixth matrix represents knowledge of the people and enterprises involved.

The red factors are explained in the sequence of credit worthiness, reputation, industry norms and state of finance.

The blue factors are explained in the sequence of worst case scenarios, diligence, respect and discipline & control.

The Reading

The red factors (in the context of getting compensation) represent the perspective and considerations of the creditors, analyzing at the potential debtors. The blue factors represent the creditors' guidelines for recovery of repayments.

This matrix deals with the basic and primary factors to be considered in the context of getting compensation. Another thing of note is the intention of the entrepreneur/enterprise to be honorable or with less than sterling intention to cheat.

 # Credit Worthiness

An honest man's word is as good as his bond.

– Miguel de Cervantes

From the business perspective, this chapter focuses on getting payment from the customers and debtors. Credit worthiness is the perception of the company held by others with regards to being worthy for credit, credit terms, credit extensions or loans. With good credit worthiness, creditors are confident that their loans will be repaid.

It is the foundation of any decision to lend to the entrepreneur/enterprise the loans or credit terms.

Good credit worthiness also impact the bargaining power of the entrepreneur/enterprise to negotiate better interest rates, the duration of credit, advantageous credit terms and more.

The general factors of credit worthiness such as the ability to repay, past performance etc. will be taken into consideration to form part of the credit worthiness of the payer.

Principle in Action

(**P**erson)

(**O**rganization)

(**W**hat Challenges)

(**E**xecution)

(**R**esults)

(**F**actors of Success/Failure)

(**U**nderstanding)

(**L**essons and insights)

The Essence: Good credit worthiness takes time to build and is a powerful tool for business dealings, do not jeopardize it.

 Reputation

A good reputation is more valuable than money.

—Publilius Syrus

Reputation is the overall judgement that others confer on you or your company since its beginning. It is the overall brand of the entire company.

Reputation can take years to build up and it can be gone in a moment. The reputation of a company begins at the same time as the birth of the company.

Reputation is the powerful perceptions associated onto the individual by his/her actions and deeds over a period of time.

Principle in Action

(**P**erson)

(**O**rganization)

(**W**hat Challenges)

(**E**xecution)

(**R**esults)

(**F**actors of Success/Failure)

(**U**nderstanding)

(**L**essons and insights)

The Essence: Reputation lost is almost an impossible task to restore.

 # Industry Norms

"A gem is not polished without friction, nor a man perfected without trials."

-Chinese Proverb

Industry norms are the performances of the average player with the other similar enterprises in the same competitive arena with the assumption of relatively strong forms of market efficiency (The relevant industry data are readily available).

<u>Principle in Action</u>

(**P**erson)

(**O**rganization)

(**W**hat Challenges)

(**E**xecution)

(**R**esults)

(**F**actors of Success/Failure)

(**U**nderstanding)

(**L**essons and insights)

The Essence: Industry norms are the standards that the various industry players abide to or uses as a benchmark for decision making process.

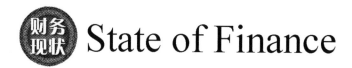

State of Finance

All wealth is the product of labor.

— John Locke

State of finance is the current position of a particular company. Referring to financial position here as in current ratio (current assets against current liabilities) and ability to pay off monetary liabilities etc.

State of finance is to be closely monitored from time to time in order to ensure that a company is having sufficient cash & cash equivalent to settle off their liabilities when they fall due.

Knowing the financial health of the company is crucial as it will prevent allowing too favorable term(s) to be negotiated at the cost of normal business operation.

Knowing the norms of the industry together with the actual financial position will help determine the pace of expansion in order to prevent over trading (unsuitable pace of rapid growth).

Principle in Action

(**P**erson)

(**O**rganization)

(**W**hat Challenges)

(**E**xecution)

(**R**esults)

(**F**actors of Success/Failure)

(**U**nderstanding)

(**L**essons and insights)

The Essence: Same business/industry, different circumstances require different measurements for accurate representations of the state of finances.

 # Worst Case Scenario

When you see a thing clearly in your mind, your creative success mechanism within you takes over and does the job much better than you could do it by conscious effort or willpower.

—Maxwell Maltz

Worst Case Scenario means the worst that can happen in any given scenario in the context of dealing with issues of debt recoverability.

The entrepreneurs/ enterprise must be sensitive to the state of finance (indicators) of customers in order to be prepared for any adverse eventuality.

The company might be suffering from significant loss if customers are not paying back in totality. If repayments from customers are delayed, then it will have an adverse effect on the company's cash flow.

Principle in Action

(**P**erson)

(**O**rganization)

(**W**hat Challenges)

(**E**xecution)

(**R**esults)

(**F**actors of Success/Failure)

(**U**nderstanding)

(**L**essons and insights)

The Essence: The entrepreneurs/ enterprise must prepared for the worst case scenarios (default/delay of repayment) in order to plan in advance should default/delay of repayment actually materialize.

 Diligence

Few things are impossible to diligence and skill.

— Samuel Johnson

Diligence means the state of applying constant effort to the task. It is also followed by the course of action after entrepreneurs/enterprises have prepared for the worst.

Diligence is equivalent to having persistence applied professionally and firmly. Hence, entrepreneurs/enterprise need not be restricted by unnecessary emotional sense of guilt/uneasiness when asking for repayment on a regular basis.

By diligently following up of amount outstanding will give the impression that the company is clear in its accounts and will strive to take constructive and effective actions.

Significant losses occur if customers have totally forgotten about the amounts outstanding due to the lack of regular and firm follow ups.

Principle in Action

(**P**erson)

(**O**rganization)

(**W**hat Challenges)

(**E**xecution)

(**R**esults)

(**F**actors of Success/Failure)

(**U**nderstanding)

(**L**essons and insights)

The Essence: Diligence is tantamount in the recovery of amount outstanding.

 # Respect

Civilization is a method of living,
an attitude of equal respect for all men.

—Jane Addams

Respect is the level of dignity and "face" that is accrued to the individual or organization. In the financial aspect, it means being professional, being polite in manners and gestures when asking for repayment. There is no benefit by losing current and potential customers by being disrespectful.

Most of the time, it is the way things were said rather than the context itself. The crux of the issue is being firm and respectful without losing the dignity and good reputation of the enterprise in the presence of picky customers (who demand unreasonable and crippling discounts in settlements) and evasive debtors.

Good relationships with the clients are essential for the survival and long term prosperity of the enterprise. Hence, collecting the amount owed by clients should not be done at the cost of causing any damages.

It is a balancing act that the entrepreneur/employees be graceful, professional yet firm with the business negotiations and repayment issues without losing decorum.

Principle in Action

(**P**erson)

(**O**rganization)

(**W**hat Challenges)

(**E**xecution)

(**R**esults)

(**F**actors of Success/Failure)

(**U**nderstanding)

(**L**essons and insights)

The Essence: Respectful yet firm is always a better way to handle business dealings.

Discipline & Control

Discipline is the bridge between goals and accomplishment.

—Jim Rohn

Discipline and control mean ensuring the principles, guidelines, strategies and plans to control the various aspects of the company with respect to demanding repayment are tightly adhered.

Entrepreneurs/enterprise must have the discipline in handling/dealing worst case scenarios mentioned above in order to seize the initiatives to control the development of the whole repayment process.

By having discipline in following the standard operating procedures, entrepreneurs/enterprise is highly likely to have the advantage to be able to control the development while directing it to the desired result in the repayment process.

Principle in Action

(**P**erson)

(**O**rganization)

(**W**hat Challenges)

(**E**xecution)

(**R**esults)

(**F**actors of Success/Failure)

(**U**nderstanding)

(**L**essons and insights)

The Essence: Be disciplined enough to adhere to proper procedures in order to control the incidents of default, discount and delay of repayments from wayward customers/business stakeholders.

Tao Zhu Gong's Business Principle 7: The Ability to Deploy People

The Seventh Business Principle— The Ability to Deploy People

There is something that is much more scarce, something far finer, something rarer than ability.
It is the ability to recognize ability.

—Thomas Jefferson

Entrepreneurs despite their resourcefulness, brilliance and skills are only human. There are real limits to the energies, time, resources and range of capabilities that the entrepreneurs have to work with. The most effective and efficient way to solve these limitations is delegation and empowerment through the professional talents that are available.

Entrepreneurs/enterprises need good, capable people (talents) to fill the positions to effectively run their businesses. The cruxes of the whole issue of delegation therefore are: getting the needed talents and deploying them well.

People are the primary resource of success for the entrepreneur/enterprise. Businesses that could not get talents and use them well, inevitably face deteriorating performances and a grim prospect as mediocre ideas and capabilities are not able to surmount the tough challenges that looms in the future.

The 13 Strategic Aspects

1. Understanding and Analysis
* *The importance, variety and the needs of talents.*

2. Acquisition of Information
* *The people, places involved with talents and employment.*

3. The Battle Environment
* *The supply of human capital.*

4. Topography of the Environment
* *The ability to attract, retain and use the talents.*

5. Weakness and Strength
* *The discoveries in the context of the abilities to attract, retain or cultivate talents.*

6. Commitment
 * *The enterprise in setting up a conducive environment for the talents to flourish.*

7. Strategic Planning
 * *The strategies and tactics used for attracting, retaining and using talents effectively.*

8. Preparation
 * *The costs of talent hunting, training and retention.*

9. Competitive Advantage
 * *The effective of the competitive advantages of the enterprise in attracting talents.*

10. The Maneuvers
 * *The in-depth analysis of the talents to discover their true strengths and weaknesses.*

11. The Engagement
 * *The deployment of the talents to appropriate positions for maximum results.*

12. The Leadership
 * *The maintenance of the talents' morale in the enterprise.*

13. Change and Adaption
 * *The constant vigilance for new talents.*

The Matrix of Tao Zhu Gong's 7th Business Principle (TZG 7th Matrix)

The Components

The core of the seventh matrix represents knowledge of the people (the talents) involved.

The red factors are explained in the sequence of objectives, capabilities, crisis management and stability.

The Reading

The red factors together form an approximate picture of whether the talent and the position are compatible.

目标条件 Objectives

A man convinced of his own merit will accept misfortune as an honor, for thus can he persuade others, as well as himself, that he is a worthy target for the arrows of fate.

— La Rochefoucauld

Objectives in the realm of talent deployment mean the set of goals and targets that the candidate must seek to achieve once assigned to the position. The clarity of the objectives and tasks ahead must not leave any doubts.

The chosen candidate is allowed appropriate levels of independence and authority to achieve his/her objectives.

Principle in Action

(**P**erson)

(**O**rganization)

(**W**hat Challenges)

(**E**xecution)

(**R**esults)

(**F**actors of Success/Failure)

(**U**nderstanding)

(**L**essons and insights)

The Essence: Be clear on the important targets that the suitable candidate must achieve.

 # Capabilities

Ability may get you to the top,
but it takes character to keep you there.

— John Wooden

The capabilities of the individual must fit the position and the following responsibilities and challenges that come with it.

Principle in Action

(**P**erson)

(**O**rganization)

(**W**hat Challenges)

(**E**xecution)

(**R**esults)

(**F**actors of Success/Failure)

(**U**nderstanding)

(**L**essons and insights)

The Essence: The capability of the individual to perform well in the assigned position.

Crisis Management

Close scrutiny will show that most crisis situations are opportunities
to either advance, or stay where you are.

—*Maxwell Maltz*

Crisis management (in the business context) is the ability to handle crises (in business) as they arise. Crises are inevitable as change transforms the rules of the business and this will bring about disruptions. The level of preparation will mitigate some of the damage and result in faster recovery.

Principle in Action

(**P**erson)

(**O**rganization)

(**Wh**at Challenges)

(**E**xecution)

(**R**esults)

(**F**actors of Success/Failure)

(**U**nderstanding)

(**L**essons and insights)

The Essence: The ability of the candidate to plan, control and transform the crisis to advantages and benefits.

 Stability

Remember that there is nothing stable in human affairs; therefore avoid
undue elation in prosperity, or undue depression in adversity.

— Socrates

Stability is focused on the abilities of the candidate to bring forth stability in various areas in times of crisis and confusion.

Principle in Action

(**P**erson)

(**O**rganization)

(**W**hat Challenges)

(**E**xecution)

(**R**esults)

(**F**actors of Success/Failure)

(**U**nderstanding)

(**L**essons and insights)

The Essence: Maintaining equilibrium throughout times of upheavals and chaos.

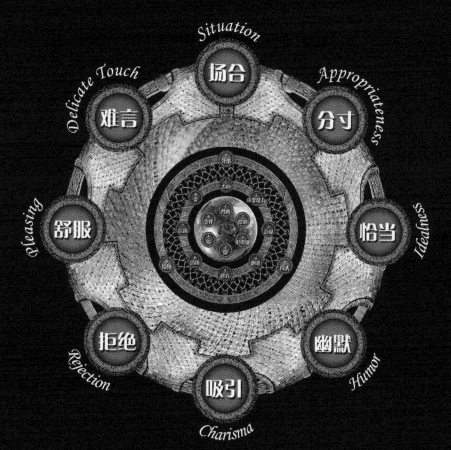

Situation
场合

Delicate Touch
难言

Appropriateness
分寸

Pleasing
舒服

Idealness
恰当

Rejection
拒绝

Humor
幽默

Charisma
吸引

陶朱公商训第八则　能辩论

Tao Zhu Gong's Business Principle 8: The Ability to Be Eloquent & Persuasive

The Eighth Business Principle—
The Ability to be Eloquent and Persuasive

You can have brilliant ideas, but if you can't get them across, your ideas won't get you anywhere.

—Lee Iacocca

Great leaders throughout history possessed high levels of mastery of their communication skills, spreading their visions and beliefs to their listeners and readers.

Opening their listeners' minds to what the vision of the future will be, instilling the faith and beliefs that are so important to make it a reality.

Communication is the bridge/pathway of ideas that leaders/entrepreneurs must learn to construct to effect changes in their followers and stakeholders.

The 13 Strategic Aspects

1. Understanding and Analysis
   * *The art and science of communication.*

2. Acquisition of Information
   * *The knowledge in books, course and the study of leaders with great communication styles.*

3. The Battle Environment
   * *The minds of people.*

4. Topography of the Environment
   * *The factors affecting the delivery and clarity of the messages.*

5. Weakness and Strength
   * *The discoveries in the context of effective communication in all aspects of business interactions.*

6. Commitment
   * *The personal desire for betterment in the realm of effective communication.*

7. Strategic Planning
   * *The strategies and tactics for communicating with various people in various settings.*

8. Preparation
- *The costs of cultivating and training to that effective level.*

9. Competitive Advantage
- *The competitive advantage(s) or benefits gained by having great communication skills.*

10. The Maneuvers
- *The training and cultivation process.*

11. The Engagement
- *The constant use of the communication skills.*

12. The Leadership
- *The level of commitment in the stakeholders sustained over time.*

13. Change and Adaption
- *The different generations of people express themselves differently.*

The Matrix of Tao Zhu Gong's 8th Business Principle (TZG 8th Matrix)

The Components

The core of the eighth matrix represents knowledge of the people (present at the business interactions).

The red factors are explained in the sequence of situation, appropriateness, idealness, humor, charisma, rejection, pleasing and delicate touch.

The Reading

The entrepreneur/leader gauging the makeup of his/her followers/stakeholders will seek to modify and adapt the presentations of the idea to the different recipient(s) for maximum impact and success rates. The red factors can be used independently or in combinations depending on the considerations faced.

 Situation

When you plant lettuce, if it does not grow well, you don't blame the lettuce. You look for reasons it is not doing well. It may need fertilizer, or more water, or less sun. You never blame the lettuce. Yet if we have problems with our friends or our family, we blame the other person. But if we know how to take care of them, they will grow well, like the lettuce. Blaming has no positive effect at all, nor does trying to persuade using reason and argument. That is my experience. If you understand, and you show that you understand, you can love, and the situation will change.

—Thich Nhat Hanh

Situation represents the events that the entrepreneurs are in.

The communication techniques, contents, timing, location are dependent on the context that the entrepreneur interact with the various people in business. It is easy to offend people with frivolous and pompous dialogues. Better to listen and think before opening your mouth.

The speech and actions must suit the situation and relevant to your goals and objectives.

Principle in Action

(**P**erson)

(**O**rganization)

(**W**hat Challenges)

(**E**xecution)

(**R**esults)

(**F**actors of Success/Failure)

(**U**nderstanding)

(**L**essons and insights)

The Essence: Act according to the strategic demands of the situation. Understand your roles and duties and act accordingly.

Appropriateness

The excellence of a gift lies in its appropriateness rather than in its value.
—*Charles Dudley Warner*

Appropriateness entails abiding to the rules of decorum in the various business situations. The golden rule is a good guideline to use when in unfamiliar formal business or socializing events.

Principle in Action

(**P**erson)

(**O**rganization)

(**W**hat Challenges)

(**E**xecution)

(**R**esults)

(**F**actors of Success/Failure)

(**U**nderstanding)

(**L**essons and insights)

The Essence: Act according to the standards and requirements of decorum.

 Idealness

It is impossible for those who are engaged in low and groveling pursuits to entertain noble and generous sentiments. Their thoughts must always necessarily be somewhat similar to their employments.

—Demosthenes

Idealness in communication is the perfection that could be achieved. It remains an ideal and a yardstick for the entrepreneur to guide his/her words.

Understanding how great speakers and business people speak in various situations about various topics will enable one to benchmark one's communication skills against them and improve upon.

History has provided multiple examples of great leaders who possessed superb leadership capabilities and the eloquence to inspire their followers to action.

Principle in Action

(**P**erson)

(**O**rganization)

(**W**hat Challenges)

(**E**xecution)

(**R**esults)

(**F**actors of Success/Failure)

(**U**nderstanding)

(**L**essons and insights)

The Essence: There is an ideal in every situation. Use that as a yardstick to discover and act accordingly.

 # Humor

In conversation humor is more than wit, easiness, more than knowledge;
few desire to learn, or to think they need it;
all desire to be pleased, or, if not, to be easy.

—Sir W Temple

Humor is a sensitive issue and a sharp double edged sword. The only safe route is to maintain one's professionalism and decorum at all times.

Even when one is familiar with the other party, best leave the joking and humor to the other party to initiate. Stay on light and proper topics.

"One man's meat is another man's poison", this saying is especially pertinent in the realm of humor.

Principle in Action

(**P**erson)

(**O**rganization)

(**W**hat Challenges)

(**E**xecution)

(**R**esults)

(**F**actors of Success/Failure)

(**U**nderstanding)

(**L**essons and insights)

The Essence: Humor can alleviate the situation with levity or dampen the situation with induced aggravation.

 # Charisma

Charm strikes the sight, but merit wins the soul.

—Alexander Pope

Charisma is a quality that magnetizes people around the possessor. Charisma is like a jigsaw puzzle of many traits and personality attributes combined.

Some people possess it naturally. Others forge it through observation of charismatic people and cultivation.

Charisma is subjective and dependent heavily on culture. Different people may react differently to the same charismatic individual. Hence it is wiser to focus on more practical skills and capabilities and add value to entrepreneur and to the success rate of the company.

Principle in Action

(**P**erson)

(**O**rganization)

(**W**hat Challenges)

(**E**xecution)

(**R**esults)

(**F**actors of Success/Failure)

(**U**nderstanding)

(**L**essons and insights)

The Essence: Charisma is simply the ability to make other feel good via their interactions with you.

 Rejection

You have to know how to accept rejection and reject acceptance.

–Ray Bradbury

In business communication, it is inevitable that one must reject the demands/ideas/proposals of others. Likewise, it is inevitable that the entrepreneur will also face rejections on a regular basis.

The entrepreneur must prepare a competitive spirit, a staunch will and clear vision to reflect on the reasons for the rejections encountered and be empowered to strive for betterment.

Principle in Action

(**P**erson)

(**O**rganization)

(**W**hat Challenges)

(**E**xecution)

(**R**esults)

(**F**actors of Success/Failure)

(**U**nderstanding)

(**L**essons and insights)

The Essence: Be gentle yet firm. Be respectful yet humane.

Pleasing

Be brief, for no discourse can please when too long.
—Miguel de Cervantes

Pleasing (in the context of communication) means that the entrepreneur/employees must be able to speak well and make it pleasurable for the other parties to communicate with him/her.

It is relatively easy to offend people nowadays. A customer may put up with your firm due to the lack of options and it is imperative to make them feel good by doing business with you. Should a competitor emerge with a competitive product/service at a cheaper price; your customers will take into account these previous encounters, buying your needed time to react strategically.

Principle in Action

(**P**erson)

(**O**rganization)

(**W**hat Challenges)

(**E**xecution)

(**R**esults)

(**F**actors of Success/Failure)

(**U**nderstanding)

(**L**essons and insights)

The Essence: Different strokes for different folks.

 Delicate Touch

Each person should see himself as though the entire world is on a delicate balance,
and with one deed, he or she can tip the scales.

—*Moses Ben Maimon Maimonides*

Delicate touch in communication represents having the mindset that understands the critical phases that occur in business interactions and communicate/act strategically and appropriately.

During the course of business, the entrepreneur has to face a series of challenging situations. Unless the entrepreneur is prepared in advance, he/she may be at a loss when the situations take a turn for the worse.

In such times, the principles and the goals of the entrepreneur are all that he/she has for guidance.

Principle in Action

(**P**erson)

(**O**rganization)

(**W**hat Challenges)

(**E**xecution)

(**R**esults)

(**F**actors of Success/Failure)

(**U**nderstanding)

(**L**essons and insights)

The Essence: Understand the fragility of the situation and the strengthening factors.

Tao Zhu Gong Business Principle 9: The Ability to Acquire Goods

THE NINTH BUSINESS PRINCIPLE— THE ABILITY TO ACQUIRE GOODS

Res tantum valet quantum vendi potest.
(A thing is worth only what someone else will pay for it.)

From the histories of every civilization, from the great entrepreneurs of the past to the present, all have one thing in common; enterprises need to manufacture goods or be in the provision of service in order to earn its keep and survive.

Entrepreneurs across the spectrum must excel in this particular principle, bringing their enterprises' competitive advantages to battle it out in this product/service arena.

To sell a product/service successfully and profitably requires the entrepreneur/enterprise to control and master the whole marketing process. For the whole process is like a chain, the strength of the chain is that of its weakest link.

The 13 Strategic Aspects

1. Understanding and Analysis
   * *The product management, marketing and supply chain management.*

2. Acquisition of Information
   * *Business literature of latest trends and development in these areas.*

3. The Battle Environment
   * *The profitability of the enterprise's offerings.*

4. Topography of the Environment
   * *The factors that affect the sales of the finished products/services.*

5. Weakness and Strength
   * *The discoveries in the context of sustaining the profitability of the product/service.*

6. Commitment
   * *The whole enterprise must be committed as this impacts the survival of the business.*

7. Strategic Planning
* *The strategies and tactics for product management, pricing, advertising and costs of the supply chain.*

8. Preparation
* *The costs of implementation and the support base.*

9. Competitive Advantage
* *The analysis of the relevance and strength of current competitive advantages.*

10. The Maneuvers
* *The constant innovations needed.*

11. The Engagement
* *The performance of sales, product mix, advertising strategies, distribution channels and the levels of profitability.*

12. The Leadership
* *The level of cohesion within the enterprise.*

13. Change and Adaption
* *The presence of new changes disrupting the conventional ways of doing business.*

The Matrix of Tao Zhu Gong's 9th Business Principle (TZG 9th Matrix)

The Components

The core of the ninth matrix represents knowledge of the markets involved, their needs and conditions.

The red factors are explained in the sequence of changes, timing, observations and people.

The blue factors are explained in the sequence of products, sales, pricing and logistics.

The Reading

The demands of the market are ever changing with time, hence the need for observations especially in the people (customers and competitors present in the markets). Directly impacting the performances of sales which in turn influence the product/selling/pricing and logistical strategies and tactics.

 Markets

"Every man lives by exchanging."

-Adam Smith

The market is the arena in which your products/services must compete with the offerings of competitors for the customers that are vital to the survival of the enterprise.

Principle in Action

(**P**erson)

(**O**rganization)

(**W**hat Challenges)

(**E**xecution)

(**R**esults)

(**F**actors of Success/Failure)

(**U**nderstanding)

(**L**essons and insights)

The Essence: A place of exchange between needs, wants, desires and the means to fulfill them. The source of the demand are the people, do you have the means to meet their demands?

 # Changes

All things change, nothing perishes.

—Ovid

Changes in the context of products/services mean the possible changes that could occur to render your offerings irrelevant and obsolete.

Principle in Action

(**P**erson)

(**O**rganization)

(**W**hat Challenges)

(**E**xecution)

(**R**esults)

(**F**actors of Success/Failure)

(**U**nderstanding)

(**L**essons and insights)

The Essence: Are you prepared to prosper on the next wave of change?

 # Timing

Observe due measure, for right timing is in all things the most important factor.

—Hesiod

Timing in this context means the timing of the launch of the new products/services. It also includes the timing of the decision to innovate and improve on current products/services.

Principle in Action

(**P**erson)

(**O**rganization)

(**W**hat Challenges)

(**E**xecution)

(**R**esults)

(**F**actors of Success/Failure)

(**U**nderstanding)

(**L**essons and insights)

The Essence: Strategic timing, ample preparations and fluid focused execution will win the day.

 # Observations

Do not believe in anything simply because you have heard it. Do not believe in anything simply because it is spoken and rumored by many. Do not believe in anything simply because it is found written in your religious books. Do not believe in anything merely on the authority of your teachers and elders. Do not believe in traditions because they have been handed down for many generations. But after observation and analysis, when you find that anything agrees with reason and is conducive to the good and benefit of one and all, then accept it and live up to it.

—The Buddha

Observations mean observing via reading the financial numbers, listening to the customers' feedback about the strengths and weaknesses of your offerings together with customer and market surveys.

Principle in Action

(**P**erson)

(**O**rganization)

(**W**hat Challenges)

(**E**xecution)

(**R**esults)

(**F**actors of Success/Failure)

(**U**nderstanding)

(**L**essons and insights)

The Essence: The changes in the mindsets and perceptions of the people that are occurring constantly.

 # People

Being deeply loved by someone gives you strength loving someone deeply gives you courage.

—Lao Tzu

People mean the customers, competitors, employees and other stakeholders of the enterprise that the entrepreneur must handle to ensure that the company can survive and prosper.

It entails managing the various relationships, their ebbs and flows and changes in their nature, the various phases and the status of the relationships.

Principle in Action

(**P**erson)

(**O**rganization)

(**W**hat Challenges)

(**E**xecution)

(**R**esults)

(**F**actors of Success/Failure)

(**U**nderstanding)

(**L**essons and insights)

The Essence: Prosper or fall by your mastery of your relationships with people.

Products

The quality will remain when the price is forgotten.

– Henry Royce

Products (inclusive of actual products and services) encompass the whole spectrum from product development to the customers actually using it. The entrepreneur is basically trying to answer the questions of:

"What products to make/sell?"

"Is it useful?"

"Will it generate profits for the enterprise?"

"How to sustain the products' profitability?"

"What is next?"

Principle in Action

(**P**erson)

(**O**rganization)

(**W**hat Challenges)

(**E**xecution)

(**R**esults)

(**F**actors of Success/Failure)

(**U**nderstanding)

(**L**essons and insights)

The Essence: Do not make mediocre products.

 # Sales

Every sale has five basic obstacles no need, no money, no hurry, no desire, no trust.

–Zig Ziglar

One of the main ways that the enterprise earns its revenues and realizes profits. Without generating a targeted volume of successful sales, the enterprise will not last long. Hence the entrepreneur is asking the basic questions of:

"How can I create the sales of my offerings?"

"How can I increase the sales of my offerings?"

"How can I sustain the sales of my offerings?"

Principle in Action

(**P**erson)

(**O**rganization)

(**W**hat Challenges)

(**E**xecution)

(**R**esults)

(**F**actors of Success/Failure)

(**U**nderstanding)

(**L**essons and insights)

The Essence: Sales follow the rhythms of the product life cycle. Act accordingly.

 # Pricing

The cynic knows the price of everything and the value of nothing.
— Oscar Wilde

The price of the product carries within the value of the product, the strategic pricing function and the profits of the enterprise.

There is a wide array of pricing strategies to fulfil the strategic objectives of the enterprise. Choosing the appropriate ones to accentuate the product/service is the crux of pricing.

Principle in Action

(**P**erson)

(**O**rganization)

(**W**hat Challenges)

(**E**xecution)

(**R**esults)

(**F**actors of Success/Failure)

(**U**nderstanding)

(**L**essons and insights)

The Essence: Your prices tell people about your products, your confidence and reveal your strategies in them.

Logistics

Concern for man himself and his fate must always form the chief interest of all technical endeavors, concern for the great unsolved problems of the organization of labor and the distribution of goods--in order that the creations of our mind shall be a blessing and not a curse to mankind. Never forget this in the midst of your diagrams and equations.

—Albert Einstein

Logistics encompasses the whole supply chain of distribution. Moving the products from the production to the customer's hands. Mastery in this will generate cost savings, adding to the financial health of the enterprise.

Principle in Action

(**P**erson)

(**O**rganization)

(**W**hat Challenges)

(**E**xecution)

(**R**esults)

(**F**actors of Success/Failure)

(**U**nderstanding)

(**L**essons and insights)

The Essence: All is futile if the product/service cannot reach the consumers.

陶朱公商训第十则　能知机

Tao Zhu Gong's Business Principle 10: The Ability to Discern Opportunities

THE TENTH BUSINESS PRINCIPLE—
THE ABILITY TO DISCERN OPPORTUNITIES

Discovery consists of seeing what everybody has seen and thinking what nobody has thought.
—Albert von Szent-Gyorgy

Opportunity is simply a potential beneficial state of being that could produce desired results when realized successfully.

Manifesting briefly due to the alignment of favorable conditions that coalesce into an invisible seed of potential success. It is up to the eagle eyed and wise entrepreneur to seize the seed and grow its potential harvest of advantages for the advancement of the enterprise.

Facing the eternal winds of change, the entrepreneur/enterprise must identify the achievable opportunities that present themselves and having prepared beforehand the means to seize them.

The 13 Strategic Aspects

1. Understanding and Analysis
- *The essence of opportunity and the ability to detect opportunities.*

2. Acquisition of Information
- *The case studies of businesses that are able to detect and seize opportunities.*

3. The Battle Environment
- *The entire business environment where innovations and opportunities manifest.*

4. Topography of the Environment
- *The factors governing the sensitivity in the detection and seizing of opportunities.*

5. Weakness and Strength
- *The discoveries in the context of the ability to detect, seize and make use of opportunities*

6. Commitment
- *The entrepreneur and enterprise in encouraging creativity and rewarding innovation.*

7. Strategic Planning
- *The strategies and methods for analyzing the feasibility of the opportunities found.*

8. Preparation
- *The costs of realizing the captured opportunity.*

9. Competitive Advantage
- *The competitive advantage(s) deployed in the capture of opportunity.*

10. The Maneuvers
- *The innovative and creative ways of analyzing from multiple angles.*

11. The Engagement
- *The constant refinement to the whole process.*

12. The Leadership
- *The adoption of unconventional but effective ways of thinking and doing.*

13. Change and Adaption
- *The potential trend that the opportunity represents.*

The Matrix of Tao Zhu Gong's 10th Business Principle (TZG 10th Matrix)

The Components

The core of the tenth matrix represents knowledge of the people involved.

The red factors are explained in the sequence of management, manpower, finances, materials, analytical tools, trends, customers, competitors, industry and changes.

The Reading

Changes are happening within all these factors simultaneously. The crux of the issue being if the level of change occurring is significant enough to affect the factor(s) to produce opportunities for the entrepreneur to capture.

管理 Management

Management means, in the last analysis, the substitution of thought for brawn and muscle, of knowledge for folkways and superstition, and of cooperation for force. It means the substitution of responsibility for obedience to rank, and of authority of performance for the authority of rank. Whenever you see a successful business, someone once made a courageous decision.

—Peter Drucker

Management is the authority/the decision makers of the company. Any changes in the management of the company hold the seeds for great change for the company.

In the competitive world of business, there exists periods of time whereby the only things that the company can do is to wait for opportunities. Opportunities in the form of chaos in the management of one's competitors will enable the entrepreneur to break out and achieve growth at the expense of the weakened competitors.

Principle in Action

(**P**erson)

(**O**rganization)

(**W**hat Challenges)

(**E**xecution)

(**R**esults)

(**F**actors of Success/Failure)

(**U**nderstanding)

(**L**essons and insights)

The Essence: The competence and confidence of the management.

 # Manpower

A man is not idle because he is absorbed in thought.
There is visible labor and there is invisible labor.

—*Victor Hugo*

Manpower represents the human resources that are available in the company. These valuable people represent capital for the enterprise to achieve success. All leaders since ancient times face the same thorny challenge of getting talented people to aid them in their quest for success.

In the modern era, it is even harder to retain people of caliber. Leaders must expend serious thoughts and efforts on talent retention. The most important points for the leaders to consider are fitting the talent into the culture of the company and appropriate positions in addition to meeting the needs of the talents to harness the full extent of their abilities.

Principle in Action

(**P**erson)

(**O**rganization)

(**W**hat Challenges)

(**E**xecution)

(**R**esults)

(**F**actors of Success/Failure)

(**U**nderstanding)

(**L**essons and insights)

The Essence: The availability of abilities matters greatly in the survival of the enterprise.

 Finances

I finally know what distinguishes man from other beasts –financial worries.

— *Jules Renard*

Finances are the lifeblood of the company. The state of finance represents the financial might of the company to survive and prosper or wither and perish. Loss of financial stability within the company is often reflective of serious disorders.

Nothing good can come out of having weak finances or being in financial troubles for an extended period of time.

Principle in Action

(**P**erson)

(**O**rganization)

(**W**hat Challenges)

(**E**xecution)

(**R**esults)

(**F**actors of Success/Failure)

(**U**nderstanding)

(**L**essons and insights)

The Essence: Fuel for growth.

 # Materials

All the means of action—the shapeless masses—the materials—lie everywhere about us.
What we need is the celestial fire to change the flint into the transparent crystal, bright and clear.
That fire is genius.

—Henry Wadsworth Longfellow

Materials in a conceptual way mean anything that can be of use to further the entrepreneur/enterprise goals and advancement. In general it refers to the resources/assets that are vital to the survival and prosperity of the enterprise.

Materials can be categorized mainly into two main broad types, tangible and intangible. The strategic entrepreneur/enterprise will strive to make the best use of its resources to achieve the best results possible.

Principle in Action

(**P**erson)

(**O**rganization)

(**W**hat Challenges)

(**E**xecution)

(**R**esults)

(**F**actors of Success/Failure)

(**U**nderstanding)

(**L**essons and insights)

The Essence: Availability of resources and their optimal deployment for success.

分析 Analytical Tools

No good workman without good tools.

—Thomas Fuller

In the course of business, the entrepreneurs must rely on numbers (in the accounts, surveys and financial reports etc.) to gauge the performance of the company and its current state.

You are what you measure. The very actual performances to measure, the tools used in the measurements, the metrics deployed, gathering the readings/numbers, running the analysis and interpretation, understanding the limitations of these analytical tools and models, all contribute to the accuracy of the big picture.

Principle in Action

(**P**erson)

(**O**rganization)

(**W**hat Challenges)

(**E**xecution)

(**R**esults)

(**F**actors of Success/Failure)

(**U**nderstanding)

(**L**essons and insights)

The Essence: You are what you measure.

 # Trends

"In the business world, the rearview mirror is always clearer than the windscreen."
-Warren Buffett

Trends are part of the business landscape and the ability to understand and capitalize on them will enable the entrepreneur/enterprise to benefit tremendously.

A trend is an ongoing process, hence the entrepreneur/enterprise must look for the critical factors that are changing in order to better adapt and adhere to the changing

Principle in Action

(**P**erson)

(**O**rganization)

(**W**hat Challenges)

(**E**xecution)

(**R**esults)

(**F**actors of Success/Failure)

(**U**nderstanding)

(**L**essons and insights)

The Essence: Having the means to see a trend, proper utilization of the trend and being able to ride the next trend.

 # Customers

"There is only one valid definition of business purpose: to create a customer."

-Peter Drucker

Changes in customers occur from the S.T.E.P. factors (chapter 3); the changes occur in their perceptions and mindsets.

Changes in customers' tastes, demands and needs. The product adoption cycle will help to gauge whether the entrepreneurs/enterprise will be able to last in the new market or just a fad.

Principle in Action

(**P**erson)

(**O**rganization)

(**W**hat Challenges)

(**E**xecution)

(**R**esults)

(**F**actors of Success/Failure)

(**U**nderstanding)

(**L**essons and insights)

The Essence: Customers are like liquids and fluids, they flow and move around.

 # Competitors

"Never compete with someone who has nothing to lose."

-Baltasar Gracian

Changes in competitors entail changes in their company's management, finances assets available capability and product performance in the market.

Any changes in them must be viewed from the entrepreneurs' own strategic view points and in relation to the nature of the relationship that exists between the competitors and the firm.

Principle in Action

(**P**erson)

(**O**rganization)

(**W**hat Challenges)

(**E**xecution)

(**R**esults)

(**F**actors of Success/Failure)

(**U**nderstanding)

(**L**essons and insights)

The Essence: Constant vigilance is the price of survival.

 Industry

"If this country is ever demoralized,
it will come from trying to live without work."
—Abraham Lincoln

Changes in industry come from STEP factors discussed in the 3rd business principle; those who cannot follow in the new environment will fold. Each new STEP developments may represent significant changes to the existing rules/norms in the industry. The entrepreneurs who prepared well in advance will survive and prosper.

Principle in Action

(**P**erson)

(**O**rganization)

(**W**hat Challenges)

(**E**xecution)

(**R**esults)

(**F**actors of Success/Failure)

(**U**nderstanding)

(**L**essons and insights)

The Essence: Sun rising or sun setting?

 # Changes

Look abroad through Nature's range,
Nature's mighty law is change.

—Robert Burns

To understand the change in changes, the entrepreneurs must understand the factors of change that could be significant to the enterprise and know how to discern and gauge the possible effects.

Principle in Action

(**P**erson)

(**O**rganization)

(**W**hat Challenges)

(**E**xecution)

(**R**esults)

(**F**actors of Success/Failure)

(**U**nderstanding)

(**L**essons and insights)

The Essence: The implications of change impacting you/your opponents.

能力
Abilities

公正
Fairness

胆略
Courage

谦虚
Humility

道德
Morals

长远
Long Term View

共患
Esprit de Corps

智谋
Strategy

忠诚
Loyalty

陶朱公商训第十一则　能倡率

Tao Zhu Gong's Business Principle 11: The Ability to Lead

The Eleventh Business Principle—
The Ability to Lead

"He who cannot be a good follower, cannot be a good leader."

-Aristotle

Leaders, they are the embodiment of the organization's visions, directions and potential destiny. Leaders are the captains of their organizations affecting the overall performance and the fates of its employees to a large degree.

Playing a vital role, leaders are being looked up to for vision, guidance and directions; hence the leader's character and principles will mold the company/organization in his/her image. The words and actions of the leaders are constantly being scrutinized by people whom they lead and by stakeholders whom they have a responsibility to, more so in this modern era of information.

A mediocre organization led by a great leader will become great in time. Unfortunately the reverse is also true; a great organization led by a poor/average leader will deteriorate and weaken.

Humans are remarkable beings of creativity and ingenuity, as such; great leadership traits and qualities can be studied in depth, distilling the vital essence for cultivation in promising candidates.

The 13 Strategic Aspects

1. Understanding and Analysis
- *The importance of leadership and the leadership qualities.*

2. Acquisition of Information
- *The historical examples of great leadership in businesses, organizations and countries.*

3. The Battle Environment
- *The present and future of the enterprise.*

4. Topography of the Environment
- *The factors that affect the quality of the leadership and the ability to guide the enterprise.*

5. Weakness and Strength
- *The discoveries in the context of recruitment, working with and the cultivation of leaders.*

6. Commitment
- *The entrepreneur and enterprise must be committed to getting good leaders.*

7. Strategic Planning
- *The strategies and methods used in talent scouting and the cultivation of leaders within.*

8. Preparation
- *The costs of the leadership cultivation initiatives and the needs of the leaders.*

9. Competitive Advantage
- *The competitive advantage(s) or benefits in the recruitment and cultivation.*

10. The Maneuvers
- *The search for the candidate with the required leadership attributes.*

11. The Engagement
- *The performance of the leaders and overall morale.*

12. The Leadership
- *The ability of the leaders to lead, empower and inspire the stakeholders.*

13. Change and Adaption
- *The choice of the next leader to lead the enterprise in the face of new challenges.*

The Matrix of Tao Zhu Gong's 11th Business Principle (TZG 11th Matrix)

The Components

The core of the eleventh matrix represents knowledge of the leaders and stakeholders involved.

The factors are explained in the sequence of morals, long term view, esprit de corps, strategy, loyalty, abilities, fairness, courage and humility.

The Reading

These are the vital factors that the leaders and potential leaders must have for the prosperity of the enterprise.

 # Morals

Leadership is a combination of strategy and character.
If you must be without one, be without the strategy.
— *Gen. H. Norman Schwarzkopf*

Morals mean the principles and integrity that a leader possess.

In times of great change, riddled with temptations, the morals of the leader will guide his/her actions and the actions of others through this trying period.

Principle in Action

(**P**erson)

(**O**rganization)

(**W**hat Challenges)

(**E**xecution)

(**R**esults)

(**F**actors of Success/Failure)

(**U**nderstanding)

(**L**essons and insights)

The Essence: Men without morals are akin to ships without compasses.

 Long Term View

The most pathetic person in the world is someone who has sight, but has no vision.

– Helen Keller

Long term view is the leaders' vision of things to come.

The vision is what guides the current planning and preparation including mobilization of resources to realize the objectives.

The vision of the leader can be viewed as the future template of the company.

Principle in Action

(**P**erson)

(**O**rganization)

(**W**hat Challenges)

(**E**xecution)

(**R**esults)

(**F**actors of Success/Failure)

(**U**nderstanding)

(**L**essons and insights)

The Essence: What is coming in the long term?

 Esprit de Corps

Alone we can do so little; together we can do so much.

—Helen Keller

Team spirit is vital for all the organization today, for no man is an island. The strength of the chain is that that of its weakest link, that is the level of competency just above failure for the team.

Due to the real limits of human, energy and resources, we must depend on teams to realize multiple objective and goals

Leaders must be able to instill team spirit. Creating a conducive environment within the enterprise to support the formation and maintenance of great teams

Principle in Action

(**P**erson)

(**O**rganization)

(**W**hat Challenges)

(**E**xecution)

(**R**esults)

(**F**actors of Success/Failure)

(**U**nderstanding)

(**L**essons and insights)

The Essence: No man is an island.

 Strategy

To conquer the enemy without resorting to war is the most desirable.
The highest form of generalship is to conquer the enemy by strategy.

—*Sun Tzu, The Art of War*

The leaders must be well versed in strategy. If the leaders are not strategic and of average capability, then the enterprise will at most achieve stable and average performance.

Strategy is anything/plan that can advance the enterprise competitive advantages. The good news about strategic mindset and skills is that it can be cultivated and strengthened.

An average leader may take over the company (the solid foundation being forged by his/her predecessors) and the company will maintain its relative strengths until the next big change.

Principle in Action

(**P**erson)

(**O**rganization)

(**W**hat Challenges)

(**E**xecution)

(**R**esults)

(**F**actors of Success/Failure)

(**U**nderstanding)

(**L**essons and insights)

The Essence: He/she who resides in the position of power and lacks strategic vision, formulation and execution will bring ruin to himself/herself, the organization and the society at large.

 Loyalty

Be with a leader when he is right, stay with him when he is still right, but, leave him when he is wrong.

—Abraham Lincoln

Loyalty in the context of leadership deals with the issues of loyalty towards the firm by the employees and even the leaders themselves.

Since ancient times, the leaders/entrepreneurs face the eternal problem of securing loyalty from their stakeholders within their organizations. In the modern era, it is even more of a challenge due to the freedom of choices and a wide variety of employment options available.

Team spirit and loyalty are the glue that holds the people together within an organization. No company can achieve internal stability without this glue and once any great challenges arise, it is easy to disintegrate.

Principle in Action

(**P**erson)

(**O**rganization)

(**W**hat Challenges)

(**E**xecution)

(**R**esults)

(**F**actors of Success/Failure)

(**U**nderstanding)

(**L**essons and insights)

The Essence: To gain the loyalty of your followers, you must be loyal to them first.

 Abilities

I am personally convinced that one person can be a change catalyst, a 'transformer' in any situation, any organization. Such an individual is yeast that can leaven an entire loaf. It requires vision, initiative, patience, respect, persistence, courage, and faith to be a transforming leader.

—Stephen Covey

Abilities are the relevant skills that the leader possesses that can add to the strategic competitive advantages of the enterprise.

Depending on the nature of the industry, enterprise, types of challenges faced, the leader will require a broad range of value adding skills to function effective and efficiently.

Principle in Action

(**P**erson)

(**O**rganization)

(**W**hat Challenges)

(**E**xecution)

(**R**esults)

(**F**actors of Success/Failure)

(**U**nderstanding)

(**L**essons and insights)

The Essence: No relevant abilities, no potential of success realization.

 # Fairness

Being good is easy, what is difficult is being just.

—Victor Hugo

The leaders must be fair in the administration of rewards and punishment. He/She must be impartial in the process to achieve respect and awe from his/her followers.

Without a sense of fairness, employees' morale will be negatively impacted. Who would give their best effort and ideas to the company under ineffectual leaders who indulged in favoritism and adverse management malpractices?

Principle in Action

(**P**erson)

(**O**rganization)

(**W**hat Challenges)

(**E**xecution)

(**R**esults)

(**F**actors of Success/Failure)

(**U**nderstanding)

(**L**essons and insights)

The Essence: Having the accurate picture of the overview and being balanced in the application of impartiality in all matters.

 Courage

Men make history, and not the other way around. In periods where there is no leadership, society stands still. Progress occurs when courageous, skillful leaders seize the opportunity to change things for the better.

—Harry S Truman

Courage is the state of mind that is empowered to move onto face the object of fear. Courage is not having no elements of fear at all, but having mastered and controlled the fear to a manageable level for bold decisive actions to be undertaken.

It takes courage to achieve anything worthwhile. The entrepreneurs needs to summon courage from deep within in order to face the legions issues in the setup of the company and during the initial developmental phases.

The entrepreneurs rely on courage to face the uncertain future. He/She must be able to instill courage in his/her people to face and embrace the new changes.

Be empowered by a sense of destiny and grounded in the mantle of responsibilities will aid in providing a stable platform of internal fortitude to stand against the challenges.

Principle in Action

(**P**erson)

(**O**rganization)

(**Wh**at Challenges)

(**E**xecution)

(**R**esults)

(**F**actors of Success/Failure)

(**U**nderstanding)

(**L**essons and insights)

The Essence: Courage supported by a strong foundation of wisdom is the key.

 # Humility

Humility must always be the portion of any man who receives acclaim earned in the blood of his followers and the sacrifices of his friends.

—Dwight D Eisenhower

Humility is the mindset and attitude that other people matters and are equal to you. Humility is the opposite of arrogance. Arrogance states that you are not worthy, does not matter in the eyes of the arrogant individual.

A humble leader views you as an equal human being whose contributions are mattered and valued.

History from all around the world has shown that arrogance in business or in war inevitably summons their downfall.

Humility is not groveling and being weak. It is the quiet confidence that the holder possess and the respect and dignity accorded to others during his/her interaction.

Principle in Action

(**P**erson)

(**O**rganization)

(**W**hat Challenges)

(**E**xecution)

(**R**esults)

(**F**actors of Success/Failure)

(**U**nderstanding)

(**L**essons and insights)

The Essence: Arrogance seeks to only alienate allies and beget new enemies.

Present
现

Negative
坏

Positive
好

Past
过

Future
未

Transformation
变

陶朱公商训第十二则 能远数

Tao Zhu Gong's Business Principle 12: The Ability to Be Far-Sighted

THE TWELFTH BUSINESS PRINCIPLE—
THE ABILITY TO BE FAR-SIGHTED

It is not the strongest of the species that survives, nor the most intelligent,
but the one most responsive to change.

—Charles Darwin

Change, a universal constant before the beginning of known time itself. Marching alongside with time, from being present in the microscopic universe of DNA and cells to the vast interstellar universe of space, change is inevitable and eternal, for everything is under its influence.

Evolution is the testament of change in living beings, constantly adjusting to adapt to the changing environments resulting in a great array of living species of plants and animals today.

In the human realm, advancements in various fields of technologies have yielded a multitude of great discoveries, new and stronger materials, better understanding of diseases and more effective cures etc.

Human beings must make peace with change. Our relationship with change must be built on the foundations of wisdom, courage and hope; the antidotes to irrational fear. Therefore allowing us to embrace the blessings/misfortunes that change bestows with equanimity and balance to achieve peace in life.

The 13 Strategic Aspects

1. Understanding and Analysis
- *The types of change coming.*

2. Acquisition of Information
- *The histories of empires built on the foundations of revolutionary discoveries and technologies.*

3. The Battle Environment
- *The relationship that exists between change and the entrepreneur/enterprise.*

4. Topography of the Environment
- *The forces of change in effect in all factors.*

168

5. Weakness and Strength
   - *The dynamics of strengths and weaknesses.*

6. Commitment
   - *The confidence and competence to face and embrace change.*

7. Strategic Planning
   - *The strategies and methods for embracing change.*

8. Preparation
   - *The accumulation of resources needed in potential ventures.*

9. Competitive Advantage
   - *The dynamics in the foundations of competitive advantage.*

10. The Maneuvers
   - *The instilling of values that welcomes changes.*

11. The Engagement
   - *The dynamics of grappling with change.*

12. The Leadership
   - *The abilities of the leaders to handle and capitalize on changes.*

13. Change and Adaption
   - *The mastery of self in the constant flux of change.*

The Matrix of Tao Zhu Gong's 12th Business Principle (TZG 12th Matrix)

The Components

The core of the twelfth matrix represents knowledge of the entrepreneur involved.

The red factors are explained in the sequence of positive, negative and transformation.

The blue factors are explained in the sequence of present, past and future.

The Reading

This matrix shows the relationships of time and the perception of events with respect to the entrepreneur. It can be applied to every aspects of the enterprise to gain insights.

 # Positive

Never let the future disturb you. You will meet it, if you have to, with the same weapons of reason which today arm you against the present.

—Marcus Aurelius

The timing, events, people, outcomes, situations, context, resources, strengths (max/optimal), weakness (min/controlled) are all working together to bring forth an advantageous state of prosperity and growth.

Principle in Action

(**P**erson)

(**O**rganization)

(**W**hat Challenges)

(**E**xecution)

(**R**esults)

(**F**actors of Success/Failure)

(**U**nderstanding)

(**L**essons and insights)

The Essence: Advantages gained by the alignment of success factors with your goals, skills, resources, planning and execution.

 Negative

Our task is not to fix the blame for the past, but to fix the course for the future.
—John Fitzgerald Kennedy

To preempt the negative events from happening, it is wise to imagine and discover as to how plans and things will go awry.

Principle in Action

(**P**erson)

(**O**rganization)

(**W**hat Challenges)

(**E**xecution)

(**R**esults)

(**F**actors of Success/Failure)

(**U**nderstanding)

(**L**essons and insights)

The Essence: Disadvantages gained by the misalignment of success factors with your goals, skills, resources, planning and execution.

 Transformation

We cannot always build the future for our youth, but we can build our youth for the future.
—Franklin D. Roosevelt

Transformation means using one's capability, resources to effect transformation of negative events into positive advantageous ones.

To effect a powerful and positive transformation, it will take the whole skill sets of the entrepreneurs, the resources of the firm and the total combined commitment and dedication of the employees to be successful.

Principle in Action

(**P**erson)

(**O**rganization)

(**W**hat Challenges)

(**E**xecution)

(**R**esults)

(**F**actors of Success/Failure)

(**U**nderstanding)

(**L**essons and insights)

The Essence: The whole process of realigning the critical factors with your goals, skills, resources, planning and execution.

 # Present

Whether it is the best of times or the worst of times, it is the only time we have.

—Art Buchwald

The Present is the state of being that exists "now". Each moment of the present is dependent/built on the foundations of choices/decisions/events faced in the past.

Principle in Action

(**P**erson)

(**O**rganization)

(**W**hat Challenges)

(**E**xecution)

(**R**esults)

(**F**actors of Success/Failure)

(**U**nderstanding)

(**L**essons and insights)

The Essence: How does your past influence your present? What are you doing now to build your future?

 # Past

"Life can only be understood backwards; but it must be lived forwards."
—Søren Kierkegaard

The past is the state of being that existed and provided the basis for the present.

Principle in Action

(**P**erson)

(**O**rganization)

(**W**hat Challenges)

(**E**xecution)

(**R**esults)

(**F**actors of Success/Failure)

(**U**nderstanding)

(**L**essons and insights)

The Essence: How do you profit from the past?

 Future

"The future depends on what you do today."

–Mahatma Gandhi

The seeds of the present deeds are the foundation of the future that has yet to come.

Principle in Action

(**P**erson)

(**O**rganization)

(**W**hat Challenges)

(**E**xecution)

(**R**esults)

(**F**actors of Success/Failure)

(**U**nderstanding)

(**L**essons and insights)

The Essence: The foundation of the future lies on the deeds and directions of the present.

EPILOGUE

Discovery consists of seeing what everybody has seen and thinking what nobody has thought.

—*Albert von Szent-Gyorgy*

Congratulations! By now, you would have experienced the ignition of insights and ideas based on the conceptual frameworks of these powerful business principles. Now, it is up to you to add to your mastery by expanding your limits through the exposure of new modern business concepts and related fields.

For example, having weaknesses in leadership capabilities; browse through the latest books on the subject and take note of the lists of skills that the authors deem important and compare that to your current skill sets. Or having jitters when asked to give a speech in front of your stakeholders? Difficulties in handling disputes amongst your employees? Use your creativity and commitment in seeking out resources for learning.

Each of these 12 principles can be a library of books on its own merit after expanding its scope to accommodate the developments and discoveries of the modern era. The first principle itself encompasses psychology, sociology and the philosophies pertaining to human natures. The sixth principle is in essence the whole financial sphere of the enterprise, including taxation, investment, accounting etc. which are out of the scope of this book.

The author adheres to explaining the principles based on their apparent applications at the time of their creation. The tax and basic accounting systems were already established in ancient China at the time of Tao Zhu Gong, yet he did not create a business principle "The ability to pay taxes" or "The ability to manage accounts". The most critical financial "ability" at that time was to be able to get paid for goods sold and services rendered, which is the focus of the TZG 6th Business Principle at first glance.

Throughout the process of writing, the author is amazed at the simple beauty of its overall conceptual framework; all the main vital aspects covered and still relevant 2500 years later. The flexibility of the framework is displayed when applied in the different business contexts. You can apply all of the Bai Gui's 4 characteristics and Tao Zhu Gong's 12 business principles in the activities of the purchasing department or in the context of recruiting people etc.

The author is overcome with gratitude at the benevolence of these wise ancients who shared their business principles freely for the benefits of future generations.

May you use these principles well and prosper.

Appendix: The List of Great Entrepreneurs as Role Models

The author recommends these entrepreneurs and businessmen as role models as a guide to the readers.

1. Bill Gates: The founder of Microsoft. The Bill and Melinda Gates Foundation.

2. Warren Buffett: The Sage of Omaha. The investment genius behind Berkshire Hathaway.

3. Dr Muhammad Yunus: Noble Peace Prize Recipient. The founder of Grameen Bank.

4. Mr. Li Ka Shing: The Superman from Hong Kong. The founder of Cheung Kong (Holdings) Limited

The reasons for the recommendations are as follows:

A. They have achieved specular successes in their own way.

B. Volumes of literature, books, documentaries detailing their lives, experiences and their struggles for success are readily available for the readers to study in depth.

C. They have donated substantial portions of their vast fortunes to charitable foundations.

D. Their vast entrepreneurial spirits and experience would enrich and ignite the readers immensely.

SPECIAL THANKS TO THE DESIGN STUDIO

I would like to thank Mrs Yeoh Pei See (email: peisyeoh@yahoo.com), from Passion Studio, based in Melaka (Malaysia) for her great skills and patience in skillfully handling my constant changes and ongoing improvements to the graphical matrices during the developmental phases. Without Mrs Yeoh's expertise, these matrices would not come into being.

BIBLIOGRAPHY

Wee, Chou Hou, "The Inspirations of Tao Zhu Gong: Modern Business Lessons from an Ancient Past", Prentice Hall, 2001.

Xu, Hui and Mint Kang, "Golden Rules: Tao Zhugong's Art of Business" Asiapac, Singapore, 2008.

Chin, Yew-Sin, "Kong Ming as Corporate Strategist", Gui Management Centre, 2001.

Khoo, Kheng-Hor, "Sun Tzu & Management" Pelanduk Publications, Malaysia, 1993.

Subash C. Jain, "Marketing Planning & Strategy 6th edition" South-Western College Publishing, a division of Thomson Learning, 2000.